John Beargrease

LEGEND OF MINNESOTA'S NORTH SHORE

John Beargrease

Legend of Minnesota's North Shore

DANIEL LANCASTER

HOLY COW! PRESS :: 2009 :: DULUTH MINNESOTA

10 9 8 7 6 5 4 3 2

Library of Congress Cataloging-in-Publication Data

Lancaster, Daniel.
John Beargrease : legend of Minnesota's North Shore / by Daniel Lancaster.
p. cm.
Includes bibliographical references.
ISBN 978-0-9779458-8-7 (alk. paper)
1. Beargrease, John. 2. Ojibwa Indians—Biography.
3. Letter carriers—Minnesota—Biography. 4. Dogsledding—Minnesota. I. Title.
E99.C6B424 2009
977.6004'973330092—dc22
[B]   2008037383

This project is supported in part by a grant award from the
Alan H. Zeppa Family Foundation, and by gifts from generous individual donors.

Holy Cow! Press books are distributed to the trade by
Consortium Book Sales & Distribution, c/o Perseus Distribution,
1094 Flex Drive, Jackson, Tennessee 38301.

For personal inquiries, write to: Holy Cow! Press,
Post Office Box 3170, Mount Royal Station, Duluth, Minnesota 55803.

Please visit our website: www.holycowpress.org

CONTENTS

PREFACE AND ACKNOWLEDGMENTS

JOHN BEARGREASE (1862-1910) was the son of a minor Anishinabe chief who presided over a small Indian community at Beaver Bay, Minnesota. Beargrease is best remembered as the celebrated North Shore mail carrier who hauled the mail by dogsled between pioneer communities along the Minnesota shore of Lake Superior. The modern-day annual John Beargrease Sled Dog Marathon is named after him.

Although the name John Beargrease is recognized statewide and famous among North Shore residents and visitors, a formal history on the remarkable man has never been written. In spite of the absence of any documented source, an abundance of apocryphal information about Beargrease has sprung up over the years. As is usually the case, the real story of John Beargrease, his family and the Anishinabe community in which he lived is more engaging than the apocrypha. From one perspective, the John Beargrease tale is the story of the settlement and development of the North Shore. From another perspective, it is the story of the Beargrease family's difficult transition from the traditional ways of their people into the modern world. Most of all, the story of John Beargrease is the simple story of a common man with an uncommonly difficult occupation.

My interest in the Beargrease story began with my children. While visiting Lake Superior, we would take turns reading Howard Sivertson's beautifully illustrated *Tales of the Old North Shore*. His depictions of John Beargrease left us wanting to know more about the enigmatic mail carrier. When we became part-time residents of the North Shore ourselves, I began to collect the local lore about Beargrease. I was frustrated to discover that, though many people had written about Beargrease, no one had ever written a biography.

In collecting Beargrease stories and anecdotes, I have often quoted my sources verbatim rather than paraphrasing them. At times, this may make for a clumsy narrative, but it was important for me to retain as many of the original North Shore voices as possible. In addition, I hoped to place the legendary mail carrier in the context of the traditional and local legends with which he grew up. Though I am not Native American, I have relied on period sources to represent Minnesota's Anishinabe (Ojibwe) culture as Beargrease would have known it. As an outsider to that culture, however,

I can only hope my depictions and interpretations are close to the mark. I am certainly not an authority on the Anishinabe, and I ask forgiveness for any misrepresentations. I hope the reader will finish the Beargrease story with a better historical scope on the white settlement of the North Shore, a deeper appreciation for Native Americans in general and Minnesota Anishinabe peoples in particular and a glimpse of the magical thread that is woven through the fabric of the North Shore.

Special thanks goes to each of the following: Anna Anderhagen, Minnesota Historical Society; Jason Burnett, great-grandson of John Beargrease; Autumn J. Conley, copy editor; J. Kay Davis, Bois Forte historian; Ellen Green, E. B. Green Editorial; Viola Keyport, granddaughter of John Beargrease; Isaac Lancaster, my comrade in microfilms; Steven and Ramona Lancaster, encouragers and proofreaders; Bill Latady, curator Bois Forte Heritage Center; Konnie LeMay, editor *Lake Superior Magazine*; Patricia Lornston, Bay Area Historical Society, Ed Maki, Jr., Bay Area Historical Society President; Rachelle Maloney, administrator Lake County Historical Society; Pat Maus, administrator Northeast Minnesota Historical Center; Jim Perlman, editor and publisher of Holy Cow! Press; Paul Purman, fellow inkling; Les Sessoms, great-great grandson of John Beargrease; Howard Sivertson, North Shore artist and author; Pat Zankman, administrator Cook County Historical Society; Marlys Zebbot, great-granddaughter of John Beargrease.

Of course, all errors, mistakes and blunders are my own, and none of the good folk named above should be implicated.

Special thanks is also due to my children, Isaac, Gabriel, Simon and Miriam for cheering me on and to my patient, long-suffering wife Maria for being patient and long-suffering over the course of the creation of this book.

Two things are certain: death and taxes. For my brother, Minnesota mail carrier David Lancaster (1952-1998), both certainties were realized on tax day, April 15, 1998. For more than a decade, David had survived the many dangers and vicissitudes of delivering the rural mail in the prairie lands of southwest Minnesota. We often worried about him as he drove through blinding blizzards and waged war against enormous snowdrifts, but somehow he always managed to push through, make his deliveries and return home. On April 15, while David was delivering the mail and collecting many-a-farmer's last-minute tax return filings, his Jeep struck a pile of gravel carelessly dumped in the road by a county crew. This book is dedicated to his memory, to the memory of mail carrier John Beargrease and to the living descendants of both men.

CHAPTER ONE

The Place of Little Cedars

A lone canoe made its way over the waves and down the shore of Lake Superior. In those days, people said "down the shore" when speaking of the direction northeast toward Grand Portage and Canada. "Up the shore" meant the direction southwest toward Superior, Wisconsin.

"Down the shore" from Superior, Wisconsin, the land as far as Canada belonged to the Anishinabe Ojibwe, the people of John Beargrease. In the past numerous treaties, revisions, renegotiations, broken promises and manipulations had forced the Ojibwe to abandon ancestral lands. Driven for generations by white expansion, the Ojibwe peoples believed at last to have found a home bequeathed to them by treaty. The United States guaranteed them the arrowhead-shaped region of Lake Superior's northern shore—land that one day would become part of Minnesota. The government gave them every rock, every stream, every lake, tree and field, every rugged cliff and winding path.

In mid-September of 1854, some Ojibwe men were camped near Old Portage, which is now the Duluth canal. Old Portage was the very border between white territory and Anishinabe land. The city of Duluth did not yet exist. The men saw the canoe on the water making its way toward them. They waved the paddlers to put in. As they suspected, the men in the canoe were whites. The Ojibwe regarded the two travelers suspiciously and asked them about their intentions. The white men explained that they were only paddling a short way down the shore to do some fishing. The Ojibwe men objected in broken English, "North Shore Indian land! White man no go!" Nevertheless, the white men went.[1]

Vestiges of the Fur Trade

White men had been down the shore before. European explorers and fur traders first began to appear in the northwoods in the seventeenth century. By the time of the Revolutionary War, French-Canadian voyageurs in the employ of the Scottish-based North West Company were already gathering every summer at the Ojibwe village of Grand Portage. The Ojibwe called Grand Portage the "Great Carrying Place," named for the long portage between the treacherous waterfalls on the Pigeon River and the harbor on Lake Superior. For a few weeks every summer, the North West Company post at Grand Portage was transformed into a great multitude. One thousand voyageurs and twice as many Indians gathered every July to exchange cargoes of peltry and trade goods.

By the mid-nineteenth century, the great fur trade empire had all but vanished from the North Shore. A few posts remained scattered here and there, and although the Indians continued to trap, the harvest was small when compared with the yields of previous generations. Beaver had become scarce, nearly extinct. Furbearers were sparse. Long gone were the days of giant piles of pelts. The great rendezvous at Grand Portage was only an old-timer's tale. More than a century of trapping had robbed the woods, emptied the streams and cleared the lakes. The paths of the old trade routes grew over. Moss covered over the blazes which once marked the trails. Only vestiges remained on the North Shore: a few white men at Fond du Lac, a few more at Grand Marais, a small trading post at Grand Portage. Except for those last few remnants, the North Shore of Lake Superior was Ojibwe land.

The Secret Missions of R. B. McLean and Thomas Clark II

In the summer of 1854, Superior, Wisconsin, was swollen with hopeful prospectors and entrepreneurs, anxiously awaiting the results from the new treaty negotiations going on at La Pointe. At stake was the entire arrowhead region. Explorers had recently discovered copper along Michigan's shores, a discovery which lead everyone to speculate that similar copper resources were probably waiting, concealed under the rocks of Lake Superior's northwest shore as well. The United States government summoned representatives of the North Shore Anishinabe to La Pointe, Wisconsin, the one-time center of the Ojibwe people, to sign a new treaty.

Even before the treaty was signed, opportunists were gathering on the border. They were eager as to bolt across the lake and stake their claims just as soon as the Ojibwe signed the new treaty. Staking claim was a matter of first-come, first-served. The business of staking settlement claims in order to secure mineral and timber rights was referred to as preempting.

The two white men paddling their canoe down the shore into Indian territory in that mid-September of 1854 were R. B. McLean and John Parry under the employ of Thomas Clark II. They were getting a head start on the preemption of Ojibwe land.

Young R. B. (Little Bob) McLean had come to Superior as a would-be preemptor seeking his fortune in the mining business. In his memoir, *Reminiscences of Early Days at the Head of the Lakes*, he explains, "There were rumors of great masses of pure copper and large veins full of copper that could be traced for long distances, but they were all on the North Shore, and that was Indian territory, white men were not allowed to enter it."

McLean found a job working for Thomas Clark II. Thomas Clark made his living as a civil engineer and surveyor in the quickly growing city of Superior, Wisconsin. He was also in the employ of the nascent R. B. Carlton Company, a group of investors who were seeking claims for mining rights on the North Shore.

In early September, just two weeks before the signing of the La Pointe treaty, Thomas Clark took McLean aside and told him to prepare for a clandestine preemption mission northeast down the shore. In his *Reminiscences*, McLean tells the story of how Clark met him on the sidewalk outside of the hotel, mysteriously told him to fetch an axe and a blanket and sent him to meet up with the old miner and explorer John Parry. When McLean found Parry, the latter explained to him, "You must not tell anyone what I tell you, but we are going to sneak over to the North Shore and try and find where those masses of copper and that big vein we have heard so much about are. Meet me at such a place, after dark, I will have the canoe and grub all ready."

McLean and Parry loaded a canoe by dark and then crossed over to the point where they hid beneath some trees until daylight. They portaged across the point, dropped the canoe back into the water and sped down the shore, hoping to escape detection. As they neared Old Portage, they were spotted by the Ojibwe men on the shore who warned them to go no further. Parry assured the Ojibwe that they were only after fish.[2]

On this first preempting expedition down the North Shore, McLean and company made several forays down the shore searching for copper, ching for anything that glittered. One trip took him as far as the old trading post at Grand Marais. If McLean had hoped to stake claims at Grand Marais, he was disappointed. Others had arrived just days before, made claims and were already building cabins. The preemptors found themselves preempted.[3]

Journey Down the Shore

A month later, the treaty of La Pointe was an established fact. The Anishinabe chiefs had agreed to surrender the land in exchange for designated reservations, compensation promises and certain other rights. The race was on. R. B. McLean set out again in a birchbark canoe. This time he went with his employer Thomas Clark. A half-breed voyageur, Jean Baptiste, served as their guide. Unlike the previous journey, this time they went by daylight, and this time they went boldly. The Indian men at Old Portage watched them pass but could no longer offer any objection. Clark kept diaries, made maps, counted the streams, measured the distances, counted the paddle strokes and sketched the shore line.

The North Shore of Lake Superior is a stone-broken land of jutting volcanic rock, sudden precipitous drops, steep climbs and clambering descents. At points, the very bedrock is scraped bare; in other places great boulders lie strewn about where they were dropped by retreating glaciers. The glaciers themselves left behind cuts and scars across the face of the land in the shape of hills, lakes and valleys.

In the days before Paul Bunyan, the North Shore was covered in virgin forest. Magnificent, rustling-leaved elm, willow, alder, black ash, maple, sugar maple and white paper birch crowded together crown-to-crown, competing for open sky. Range after range of forested hills, cedar, white cedar, pine and red pine, white pine and spruce standing straight and towering, like an endless maze of columns and pillars. The trees rose into the sky fifty, seventy-five, one-hundred feet or more. Half the way to their peaks, their branches spread out overhead to create a ceiling of thick needles sunlight scarcely pierced. The conifers had trunks so wide around that two men together could not span their circumference.

Clark stepped ashore and into the woods and declared in his journal, "The forest is a perfect mat of entwined underbrush—cedar & savin boughs ... To go into the country 'prospecting' would be fruitless as I could not progress over 3 or 4 miles in a day ..."[4]

The trees would not hold him back, though. In his mind, Clark saw logging camps and sawmills. He imagined meadows, cattle grazing, crops and fields, abundant harvests, wealthy farmsteads, settlements, towns and cities.

On October 20, Clark, McLean and Baptiste paddled their canoe into a pleasant twin bay at the mouth of the *Gajigijikensikag*—the Little Cedar River. Clark wrote in his diary, "These two bays are the best [harbors] I have yet found—if mineral and fishing are good—it is a desirable place."[5]

They continued down the lake toward Grand Marais. Clark made notes about the shoreline. He wrote about the cliffs of Palisade Head, "beautifully grand, raising from—no soundings or very deep water—at least 200 feet, some say 300... red columnar rock." He described the Baptism River where McLean tried trout fishing. He described paddling through the fog to land at Little Marais where he found "two huts, one or two years old—the remains of wigwams." Bad weather pinned them down a few days somewhere near the Caribou River. Clark wrote, "One accustomed to heavy weather with steamers and other large craft, feels quite uneasy in a bark canoe 500 feet from a rock bound shore with the seas running 5 or 6 feet height, & occasionally an 'old one' letting him down in the trough out of sight of land, & then up as upon a haystack—but with such men as I have, 'Little Bob' at the helm & Baptiste at the oars, all are as safe as safe can be, with a half inch of birch bark between one and Davy's Locker..."[6]

While McLean fished for supper and Baptiste made camp, Clark could be found jotting in his journal about the timber and mineral potential of each place they stopped along the shore. "The rock is magnetic, a piece weighing 4 ounces attracts the compass needle 10 degrees," he wrote on October 26.[7]

On the trip back up the shore toward Superior he described Carlton Peak, "an isolated Bluff towering its head about 700 feet ... tho' not so high as many others passed today—but in standing alone will render it a marked land object for the sailor & voyageur."[8] They stopped at Cross River where he reported finding the remains of Father Baraga's original cross. Later the same day, they encountered Ojibwe. Baptiste served as translator. They traded salt pork for trout with them.

The Beaver River

Nine days after having left the double harbor at the mouth of the Little Cedar River behind on their way northeast, they returned to explore the "desirable place." They examined the falls and the trees—pines, black ash, birch, elm, spruce and white cedar. They noted the proud rock formations and the fine meadow land. Clark was dreaming dreams and hatching schemes. He could visualize sawmills and copper mines.

He wrote, "This little Bay is a good shelter for any but an east wind and even that may be sheltered against by one or two vessels. Among the floodwood brought down by the river I find wood cut by beaver, sticks from 2 to 4 inches in diameter, 6 inches to 2 feet long—cut as smooth as a boy would with a dull axe. No doubt [the beavers] may be found within a few miles up the river."[9]

The next day, Clark and McLean set out to find the beavers and whatever else they might discover. They told Baptiste to take the canoe and wait for them up the shore at the mouth of the Split Rock river. In the meantime, they shouldered their packs and explored several miles of the Little Cedar River inland. In his *Reminiscences*, McLean recalled following the valley of the river through a large body of white pine that stood along both banks. "Enough to keep a mill running for a number of years," he wrote.[10] The timber impressed Clark, too. In his journal, he wrote, "Timber pine & Birch. Good Pines all the way thus far along the creek & as far each way as I can see … spruce bluff, ash, good pine …"[11] Some distance upstream he described a great beaver dam across the river. "I cross it. It is brush covered. Sand & gravel raising water about 3 feet. The water gently glides over it evenly. Lodged upon it are the sticks before noted, the bark eaten off. They have cut trees as large as 1 foot through—black ash & birch, & eaten the twigs."[12] That is how the Little Cedar River came to be called the Beaver River, and the bay that the Ojibwe had called "Place of Little Cedars" came to be called Beaver Bay.

Clark staked claims near the mouth of the river, and they returned to Superior. He immediately sent McLean and two other men back to the river to build three cabins on the site. By law, the cabins would hold down the water and timber rights. It was already late in the year when the three men began to build the cabins, and the winter of 1854 came early and cut them off from civilization. The December waters of Lake Superior were not safe to navigate, and the three men did not think much of hazarding an overland trek through snow and wood.

The lay of the land made travel up and down the shore difficult enough in the summer. In the cold and ice-locked winters, heavy snows piled themselves up one after another, ever deeper. Temperatures dipped low and lower until a man's toes and fingers might be frozen off. Then came the rolling fog and mist from the lake, freezing like a layer of glass over every rock and twig. The ice turned the whole world crystal, glistening and unreal. If the snows were deep, travel across country was virtually impossible except by snowshoe. A man might attempt to wade through the knee-deep (sometimes waist-deep) snow, but he would find each forward step utterly fatiguing. Instead of risking their lives, they waited, hoping their supplies could be made to last. They got lucky. The temperature dropped even more; the lake froze, and they walked back to Superior across the surface of the ice.

The Wieland Brothers

Christian Wieland, the second oldest of five German brothers, worked for Thomas Clark as civil engineer and surveyor in Superior. After staking his claim at the Beaver River, Clark began the work of platting out his imaginary town. He turned to Christian Wieland for assistance. Wieland visited the town site and was so impressed with its potential that he wrote to his brothers in Ohio, advising them to sell the family tannery at once. They did so, and, in June of 1856, the Wieland brothers bought and took possession of all the rights and interests that Clark and his associate pre-emptors had at Beaver Bay. That same summer, Henry, Albert and August Wieland chartered the side-wheel steamer *Illinois* to carry them and some twenty-two other German-speaking passengers, including Henry's wife Rosine and their two small children, to the North Shore of the lake. The *Illinois* anchored as near to shore as possible. The crew of the steamer lowered their passengers in life boats. Livestock and horses were lowered over the side by ropes and forced to swim to shore. On the shore Thomas Clark and his wife were waiting to welcome the settlers: the Wielands, John Gilomes, Tishers, Nicklars, Shaws, Christs, Domes and others. Within a year, Christian and Ernst, the other two Wieland brothers, made their homes at Beaver Bay as well.

Two months after the initial Wieland landing, the traveling Methodist missionary James Peet was on the North Shore spreading Methodism to the Ojibwe. He came across the new settlement of Beaver Bay and stayed with the Germans there for a short while. In his diary, he observed their progress:

Beaver Bay has three cabins and two families. Post office is here. Slept on floor of store at Beaver Bay… It is seven weeks today since this colony of Germans landed at Beaver Bay, since which they have made their land 'claims,' built two shanties, seven houses, chopped twelve acres, four of which they have got in crops. Made seven miles of road, cut twelve tons of wild hay, and they hope to find grass for fifty to one hundred tons.[13]

The Wieland brothers took claims along the Beaver River, each one acquiring a homestead of 160 acres, the maximum amount allowable under the homesteading laws. Henry and his wife Rosine selected a site along the river five miles from the village in an area they called West Beaver Meadow. Henry raised a log home for them. He split shingles by hand with a broad axe. He cut boards by hand with a large handsaw. He cleared the Beaver Meadow and tilled up the soil for a garden across the river. They traversed the river by way of a large log which served as a natural bridge.

Beaver Bay Indians

In the summer of 1858, Rosine left her two sons (a three-year-old and a five-year-old) playing in the yard while she crossed over the log bridge to tend the garden. Glancing back to check on her children, a wave of terror washed over her. "She saw some Indians 'in full war regalia' near them."[14] In a blind panic, she rushed for her children, lost her footing on the log bridge and plunged into the river. Ordinarily, a dip in the Beaver River might not be a serious matter, but heavy rains can transform it into a rushing torrent, and Rosine could not swim.

Who was the more startled? The frightened German woman who saw what she must have assumed to be dangerous savages near her children, or the curious Anishinabe men who watched this shrieking mad woman drop into the river like a stone. Regardless of their finery, paint and feathers, one of the men leapt into the water to rescue the struggling woman.

That same summer, two Anishinabe families—the Anuquettes and the Morrisons—built wigwams on the gravel peninsula at the mouth of the river.[15] Anuquette's Ojibwe name translated to "Cloud." John Morrison was a half-breed. They stayed the summer, hunting, trapping and fishing. They found that they could trade to an advantage at the general store and enjoyed the benefits the settlement had to offer, but they returned to Grand Portage that fall.

Otto Wieland suggests that the Ojibwe "had come to Beaver Bay off and on for many generations and knew the region well."[16] For the first several years of the settlement, however, none resided at Beaver Bay. The settlers considered the two wigwams on the peninsular point a fluke. They did not anticipate that within twenty years, Indians would constitute nearly forty percent of the population of Beaver Bay.

The next spring, the Indians returned. The settlers were surprised to see several birchbark canoes round the rocky coast and glide into the bay. The canoes were loaded heavily, their gunwales only inches above the water. One after another they beached on the gravel peninsula at the mouth of the river. Then the families began the business of extricating themselves from beneath bundles of supplies and belongings. Each canoe contained a man, his wife, several children, a pile of birchbark baskets, deerskin packages, a dog or two, and whatever else belonged to the family. Within a day or so, several more wigwams were standing on the peninsula.

The Beaver Bay Indians were mostly from the Grand Portage band. They were known as the Clan of the Bear. Only a small number of the Grand Portage band actually lived on the Grand Portage reservation that the Treaty of La Pointe had allotted to them. The rest were scattered about in small clans. The Caribou clan settled at Grand Marais. The Crane clan dominated Grand Portage. The Beaver Bay Indians were predominantly of the Bear clan.[17] The 1860 Federal Census lists Paul Musquish as the leader of the Beaver Bay Band, a relative of Louis Maymushkowaush, a chief from Grand Portage and one of the signers of the Treaty of La Pointe.

Within five years, several more Anishinabe families had joined the Beaver Bay community. The Makasabetows, the Shotlows, the Sakakees, the Naganabs, the Yellowbirds, more Morrisons, and the Wishcops. Sometime after 1870, Chief Beargrease, the father of John Beargrease, arrived with his wives and children. Within another decade, forty-one Indians and sixty-five whites lived in Beaver Bay.

Good Neighbors

A great financial panic in 1857 resulted in settlers up and down the North Shore abandoning their claims and a large portion of the Beaver Bay settlers left with them. Davis points out that several of the original German settlers were farmers, hoping to make agriculture work at Beaver Bay. Two years of working shallow, rocky soil in a short, cold growing season taught them otherwise. The 1860 Federal Census lists more than fifty unoccupied residences in Beaver Bay, but the influx of half-a-dozen or so Indian families boosted the population. Even more importantly, the Indians brought with them the skills necessary for survival in the north-woods. The Beaver Bay Germans were not outdoorsmen. Hunting and trapping did not come naturally to them, and they quickly found them-selves beholden to the master hunters and fishermen living among them to complement their potato diet. Young H. P. Wieland, the son of Henry and Rosine, recalled, "The only food there was for years, was potatoes and fish with a rabbit or a partridge once in awhile. Not to forget wild ducks and passenger pigeon. I know many days that we had fish and potatoes for breakfast, potatoes and fish for dinner and the left-overs for supper. There was always plenty of milk. Bread was a luxury; fruit out of the question but we were all healthy and contented."[18]

The Anishinabe knew the northwoods for good hunting and abun-dant fish. They used the paper-birch for wigwams and canoes. They tapped maple sap for sugar and syrup. They knew the seasons for gathering blue-berries, raspberries, chokeberries, juneberries and cranberries. They hunted caribou, moose, bear and the occasional deer or elk.

Davis writes, "The very lives of the pioneers were often dependent upon the Indian experience and knowledge of woods and weather."[19] The North Shore possesses a particularly unforgiving climate, better suited for growing pine trees than crops. The long winters isolated the settlers from civilization and supplies. No roads had yet been cut, and the heavy snows made travel impossible except by snowshoe and dogsled. The Anishinabe, on the other hand, were well accustomed to the cold months on Lake Superior. They shared their survival skills with the settlers, taught them to hunt and trap, taught them the way of the snowshoe and taught them to track game and set traps.

Helen Wieland Skillings writes about the relationship:

> The Indians were good neighbors, honest and trustworthy. They would share the spoils of the hunt with the settlers, often bringing them part of a caribou or bear meat. Caribou were abundant at that time in northern Minnesota. Beaver meat, the tail of which was delicious, although quite fat, also was presented to the settlers.[20]

The settlers remunerated the Indians for the game meat by trading with them. H. P. Wieland recalled hunting and trapping in winter, skills he had learned from the Beaver Bay Ojibwe:

There were beaver, otters, mink, martin, fisher, lynx, fox, muskrats, weasels and skunks. The prize for muskrats and weasel was so low in those days that it did not pay to hunt them. The skunks had such a strong odor that no one wanted anything to do with them. There were also moose and caribou.[21]

Wieland goes on to observe that the white-tailed deer which now overrun the North Shore were rare in those days.

Cross-Cultural Beaver Bay

An exchange of cultures took place. The Ojibwe men taught the white men the ways of the land. The whites offered the Ojibwe employment. The Ojibwe women assisted the white women in all manner of chores and became the village babysitters. Many white babies spent their early days nestled in the snug embrace of the *tikinagan*, the traditional Indian cradle.

The German-speaking settler-children of Beaver Bay learned Ojibwe before they learned English. At the age of thirteen, H. P. Wieland (the son of Henry and Rosine) spent a winter alone at Greenwood Lake to trade with Indians because he could speak fluent Ojibwe.[22] The Ojibwe, in turn, learned German and English.

Young John Beargrease and his siblings grew up with one foot in the old world of their fathers and the other in the new world of the settlers. They shared the playground of the woods, the rocks, the river and the lake. "The Indian boys and girls were born swimmers, handling themselves very skillfully in the cold water of Lake Superior, whereas the white children limited their swimming to the warmer waters of the river."[23] Anyone who has taken a dip in the frigid water of Lake Superior, even in the warmest weeks of July and August, can appreciate the white children's reluctance to swim in the lake. The Anishinabe, however, reveled in challenge, and even as children they met every test of endurance with zeal. The white children looked at the Indians for all their manifold skills and prowess with wonderment and admiration. Likewise, the Ojibwe children esteemed the whites for their fine homes and clever implements in high regard. In the earliest years, the Indian children did not attend school. Their school was the school of the old paths, the ways of their fathers and mothers—the simple wisdom of survival. As a result, John Beargrease and his siblings grew up illiterate.

Beargrease himself never attended a day of school. His younger brother Peter attended school for five days before giving it up forever. Nevertheless, in observing their white peers, those sons and daughters of the original Beaver Bay Indians recognized the value of education. When it came to raising their own children, they eagerly sent them to school along with the white children.

The Beaver Bay community did have things to offer the Anishinabe families. As some of the early, less tenacious settlers abandoned their cabins, Indian families took them over. The Wieland's built new houses for other Indian families in the community. Eventually, even the wigwams on the peninsula were replaced by wooden homes.

For the Anishinabe families, one of the great attractions of Beaver Bay was the Wieland's general store with its wide array of merchandise. Before the Mayhew's opened their trading post in Grand Marais, and before the boomtown of Two Harbors sprang into being, the Wieland store was the only supply post between Grand Portage and Duluth. Although it was a store and not a trading post, the Indians brought furs as currency. They found that the honest Germans of the community gave them fairer trades for their peltry than they might get elsewhere. Even still, before doing business, protocol demanded a long smoke:

> The Indians would not consider doing any business until they had had a smoke. Having spent the winter months trapping and hunting in the woods, their supply of good tobacco would be exhausted, and they would have to resort to their own mixture called kinnikinnick. This was made from the dried leaves or bark of the red willow and red dogwood and proved a fairly good smoke. The storekeeper would provide them with good tobacco. Arraying themselves along the walls of the store, in squatting fashion, and wrapping their blankets about them, they would fill their big pipes, and bow their heads between their knees. After smoking several pipes, they would be ready to transact their business.[24]

Trade aside, the white settlers and Indians found fellowship on other occasions as well. In 1952, Carrie Hangartner-Betzler (born in 1870) recalled that as a young girl in Beaver Bay "an annual event was a celebration we put on for [the Indians] every New Year's."[25] The same custom was practiced all along the North Shore. Every New Year's Day was called "Visiting Day." The settlers would dress in their finest and prepare cookies, cakes and treats. The Indians spent the day going from house to house in small groups. Once invited in, they would sit on the floor and make conversation with their hosts, who, in turn, filled their bags and sacks with all sorts of goodies. The *Cook County Herald* never failed to comment on the

New Year's Day tradition in Grand Marais, noting that the custom transformed New Year's into the biggest holiday of the year. The extra money generated by the annual Indian payment stipulated by the Treaty of La Pointe, payable at New Year's, only added to the fun and festivity. The occasion was thoroughly enjoyed by the hosts as much as it was by the guests.

The Schooner *Charley*

The settlers, overall, were grateful for the Indian presence. The relationship was mutually congenial, and the whites were obliged to the Indians for the game meat they brought to the village. If the Wieland brothers were a bit short in the rudiments of hunting and trapping, they did, however, understand business and progress. Within a few years of settling, they had built a water-powered sawmill at the foot of the second waterfall on the Beaver River and had already begun logging off the timber along the banks. They employed teams of men to fell the trees and haul the logs by ox-drawn sleds. The Indians living on the peninsula found employment in their small lumber camps and at their sawmill.

The Wieland brothers sold the first of their cut lumber locally. The residents of Beaver Bay quickly replaced their log cabins with fine, sturdy homes. As Beaver Bay could not provide a market large enough to sustain a lumber and sawmill operation, the H. Wieland & Brothers Lumber Company of Beaver Bay, Minnesota, began exporting their lumber to Michigan. To ease export, they purchased a two-masted schooner they named the *Charley*.

Though the *Charley* was a new vessel when the Wielands purchased it, they affectionately referred to it as "that faithful old tub." In the early years of her operation, the faithful old tub was one of only three schooners in general service on Lake Superior. For the residents of Beaver Bay, their own graceful schooner made a sight as she glided in and out of the double-harbor.

Local men, including the Anishinabe, served onboard. The crew was seldom less than half-Indian. Albert Wieland became the master and commander of the vessel. While tossing about in the wind and waves of Lake Superior, he shouted his orders to the crew in a mixture of German, English and Ojibwe. In later years, the old settlers "used to delight in attempting to repeat the inimitable conglomeration of Chippewa, German and English in which Captain Albert invariably called out his commands."[26] Chief Beargrease, John Morrison and Antoine Mashowash—all prominent men of the Indian community—served as officers of sorts. In later years, young John Beargrease served as a deck hand and pilot as well. The able crew of the *Charley* delivered lumber to ports all along the Lake.

The young Beargrease children must have felt a rush of enthusiasm as they saw the *Charley* round the point, bringing their father home after a week or so away. In Anishinabe culture, people do not do a lot of shouting and waving on such occasions. More than likely, the Beargrease children and their playmates stood silently, watching intently while the crewmen tossed ropes to the dock hands and the schooner was secured. Despite the quiet welcome, their excitement was no less than that of white children with all their waving and shouting.

From May to mid-December, the *Charley* ran back and forth on the lake. She carried more than lumber. She was also laden with the produce of Beaver Bay: potatoes, cabbage, sauerkraut and Beaver Bay's very own vintage raspberry wine.[27] During the winter months, the Wieland brothers harbored her in Duluth until the ice was open and the waves were calm in late April or May.

Lake Superior is notorious for sudden storms and tragic shipwrecks. In the two decades of her life on the lake, the *Charley* must have endured innumerable storms, sudden northeasters that transformed the surface of the lake into a frigid, churning cauldron. Those on board earned their sea legs. Through many-a-storm, they blistered their hands pulling on wet ropes and purified their souls praying for mercy. Chief Beargrease and his sons worked the ropes, slipping along the icy deck in the spray of the waves. It is a credit to the competence of the crew that the only two wrecks the ship suffered (until her unfortunate end) were minor—driven aground once at Madeline Island and once at Grand Marais, Michigan.

On May 10 of 1881, however, the *Charley* met with disaster. It was early in the shipping season, perhaps too early. The *Charley* was on her first trip from Duluth to Beaver Bay when a dreaded northeaster came rolling down onto the lake. Confident that they could still make the harbor at Beaver Bay, the crew guided their ship in, despite the roiling waves and driving wind. They made the mouth of the harbor just as they had hoped, but the intensity of the storm had grown, tossing up even the shallows of the harbor. Nevertheless, the crew reached the dock and urgently sought to tie the ship down. Before a dock hand arrived to catch the ropes and secure the ship, the waves tore the *Charley* away and tossed her up broadside on the beach where she was quickly dashed to pieces. Young H. P. Wieland and his wife were on board. They walked from the wreck to their home at the mouth of the river.[28]

Eleven years before the *Charley's* demise, Mrs. J. J. Lowry captured it in a painting she made of Beaver Bay. The painting depicts the schooner coming to dock at the mouth of the Beaver River. Four wigwams are visible on the peninsula.[29]

Winter Rescue

In very cold years in late January and February, the water along the shores of Lake Superior freezes. When it does, it provides travelers the rare luxury of a level surface on which to travel. In the days of John Beargrease, this freezing facilitated faster mail runs. As often as the ice allowed him, the mailman abandoned the wild and twisting trails for the quick, smooth surface of the frozen lakeshore. The lake ice, however, can be treacherous and deceitful. A shift in the direction of the wind and waves might suddenly break up seemingly solid ice. In other areas, a patch of thin ice might lie concealed under the snow.

On one such occasion, a Wieland brother and one of his nephews had opted to try the ice in order to save time and effort as they set out on some errand. While Davis does not specify which Wieland this was, it is probable that it was Albert Wieland and his nephew Henry P. Wieland, the son of Henry and Rosine. "Uncle Albert was the mail carrier, and as soon as I was old enough I often accompanied him,"[30] H. P. Wieland recalled. They made very good time on the ice and were more than twenty miles up the shore (southwest) when, suddenly, they both broke through the ice. Fortunately, they were able to pull themselves out of the frigid water, but almost immediately they broke through the ice again and then again. Soaked to the bone and utterly chilled, freezing stiff in the cold air, the wearied travelers climbed up the shore at the mouth of the Encampment River.

Meanwhile, back in Beaver Bay, the time of their expected return came and went. Their long absence was noted with growing concern. When at last it became clear that the two had met with some misfortune, the Wielands prevailed upon some of the young Ojibwe and persuaded them to form a search party. The men agreed, packed up some food, and set out on the trail of the two settlers. They found them, warmed them, fed them and returned them to their families at the Place of Little Cedars.

CHAPTER TWO

Moquabimetem

In 1854, four chiefs from Grand Portage, Shaganasheence, Addikonse, Waywegewam and Maymushkowaush, joined several other Ojibwe representatives to negotiate with the U.S. Government at La Pointe, Wisconsin. This was the very same treaty negotiation that R. B. McLean and Thomas Clark were salivating about while making their clandestine preemption missions. Addikonse, the chief of the Caribou band refused to budge under government pressure. His stern bargaining won payments worth $19,000 a year for twenty years in addition to reservation lands within their own territory. The annuity payments were initially meted out annually at Grand Portage. Every year the scattered clans of the Grand Portage and Bois Forte bands converged on Grand Portage. The event became a sort of festival, a new Grand Portage rendezvous. Within a decade of the signing of the treaty, more than 1,400 people were coming together at Grand Portage to await the arrival of the Indian agent's boat.[1]

One small settlement of Ojibwe, however, had not heard about the treaty or the annuity payments. The oldest record relating to the Beargrease family is an annuity report in which an Indian agent tells of discovering a community of ninety-seven Chippewa, the "Bear Grease Band of the Bois Forte Indians" living in isolation near Prairie Lake.[2] Prairie Lake is in St. Louis County near modern day Cloquet, MN. The Ojibwe called it *Hush-kodensiwi*, meaning "Little Prairie."[3]

The Beargrease Band living at Little Prairie had never taken annuities, nor were they living with their tribe, the Bois Forte, when the government stumbled upon their community. The Indian Agency immediately set to work relocating them into reservations, enticing them with annuity payments, agricultural implements and land on the newly formed Fond du Lac reservation. In a letter to the commissioner of Indian affairs in Washington, D.C., the Chippewa Lake Superior Indian Agent S. N. Clark reported, "For several years this Band has been separated from the other Indians under Gabishdodaway and spend most of the time in the vicinity of Prairie Lake a few miles beyond the boundaries of the St. Louis Reservation…"[4] The letter went on to report that the Beargrease Band was willing to relocate to the St. Louis Reservation. The Indian agent promised the band agricultural implements and assistance in transitioning to an agricultural life if they would relocate.

Chief Moquabimetem[5] must have been one of the Ojibwe discovered at Prairie Lake. Moquabimetem means "Beargrease." Chief Moquabimetem was born in the Rainy Lake district of Minnesota, circa 1830.[6] He and his kin were members of the Bois Forte tribe and had family connections within the Nett Lake band of Ojibwe and the Grand Portage band.

A second chief from Prairie Lake by the name of Mahjeheshig also went by the name Beargrease. According to former Bois Forte historian J. Kay Davis, they were brothers, the younger siblings of the chief of the Grand Portage tribe.[7]

Mahjeheshig took the Indian agent's offer and moved his family onto the reservation.[8] His brother Moquabimetem did not take the government's offer to settle on the reservation.[9] Instead he relocated to the North Shore, eventually arriving at Beaver Bay where he found the Bear Clan already living. The community at Beaver Bay welcomed him and honored him as a chief.

The Chief and His Wives

Chief Moquabimetem and his family settled in Beaver Bay sometime between 1870 and 1875. He was in his early forties. "A tall stately man, my mother called him a noble character," Helen Wieland Skillings recalled.[10]

Moquabimetem must have been a noble character. He had at least two wives, when he arrived in Beaver Bay, and he took more before he died. In his culture at that time, polygamy was a sign of prowess, nobility and social stature. The more clever and successful a hunter was, the more wives he had. A man who was able to bring home an abundance of game could scarcely ward off additional wives. The community regarded a hunter who could support several women as a man of exceptional gifting, and parents were always offering such a man their daughters.[11]

Skillings goes on to say, "Of his many wives two always accompanied him. One was a tall, very neat woman, the other a small unkempt looking woman."[12] An 1875 State Census report from Beaver Bay identifies the two women as Newigagamibig and Bidwivegamibag. Newigagamibig was the taller of the two and is believed to be the mother of John Beargrease, who is reported to have stood six feet tall himself. Other sources name her Otoe—probably a nickname.[13] A 1905 State Census of Beaver Bay provides her with the English name Nancy. Like her husband, she was in her early forties when she arrived in Beaver Bay with him, his other wife, and their large, collective brood.

Like his famous son after him, Chief Moquabimetem seems to have also been known by the English name John. His Ojibwe name translates literally as "bear-grease." The name sounds odd to modern ears, but in Native American culture, bear-grease was an important commodity with a multitude of applications. The Ojibwe used bear-grease for cooking, conditioning hides, slicking and grooming hair, waterproofing, face painting (when mixed with pigments), lubricating, greasing, protecting from frostbite, and in rancid form or mixed with skunk-oil they applied it as insect repellent. The white population prized bear-grease as well. In the mid-nineteenth century, cosmetic manufacturers were bottling bear-grease and selling it as a cure for baldness. A whole new world of balding white men relied on the skills of bear hunters and trappers to procure for them the precious commodity. A typical newspaper advertisement from those days states, "Of all preparations for the hair or whiskers, nothing equals the oil prepared from Bear's Grease. In most instances, it restores the hair to the bald and will effectually preserve it from falling off in any event."[14]

Chief Beargrease seems to have inherited his name from the Beargrease band of Ojibwe, or perhaps the Beargrease band was named after the chief's family. Originally, the name Beargrease may have been given to celebrate the exploits of some young brave bear hunter, or perhaps the Beargrease band was so-named for their unique relationship with the spirit of the bear—a family icon of sorts. The Ojibwe regarded bears as the most clever of the forest animals.

Beargrease and the Bear

Chief Moquabimetem did have at least one encounter with a bear shortly after settling in Beaver Bay. H. P. Wieland tells the story in his *Reminiscences*:

> Mokquabemmette (Beargrease) was on his way to Beaver Bay in March 1870, when he spied Moqua (bear), sunning himself under a large spruce tree. Because of thawing weather, the bear was unable to move fast in 3 feet of soft snow. The bear looked like good meat to the Indian, who unfortunately did not have his gun with him. He decided to take a 10-foot stick, tie his butcher knife to it, and stab the bear to death. But all this did was to tickle the bear. Seeing that this would not work, the Indian cut a club from a birch sapling with his tomahawk and tried to kill the bear by clubbing him. In drawing back for the first blow, he became entangled in the limbs of a tree and fell. Now came Moqua's turn to attack. He jumped on the Indian, clawing his arm and shoulder badly. The bear finally left the Indian, who was unconscious. According to the Indian's story, this must have been about three o'clock in the afternoon. When he regained consciousness, it was night. He was a very sick man and half frozen. He managed to get to the farm of Jacob Hangartner, who after warming and feeding him, brought him to Beaver Bay. The Indian suffered more from exposure than from the bear's attack. After a few weeks of good care Beargrease was able to go home. Three of us started at once to get the bear. The thermometer that night went to zero and the wet snow froze so hard that the bear got away.[15]

The story was also remembered by Carrie Hangartner (Mrs. John Stein), who was a young girl at the time.[16] She recalled the night the strange, injured houseguest came. She remembered particularly how the Indian preferred to sleep on the floor with an inverted dish pan for a pillow while he recuperated.[17]

Because Chief Moquabimetem went by the English name John Beargrease, he is inevitably confused with his famous son. Several local histories mistakenly attribute the story of his encounter with the bear to his son John.

Christmas Cookies

The white settlers of Beaver Bay had to learn to adjust to living with Ojibwe neighbors. Cross-cultural communication is always difficult and fraught with potential faux pas. Helen Skillings tells a humorous Chief Beargrease story that well illustrates the perils of cross-cultural misunderstanding. The story involves Rosine Wieland, the woman who originally fell off of the log and into the Beaver River when the first Anishinabe men appeared in Beaver Bay.

A few days before Christmas, Mrs. Henry Wieland had finished the Christmas baking, consisting of an assortment of delicious cookies including the traditional German *springerle* and *lebkuchen*. These were to have lasted her family for some time. [Chief] Beargrease must have had an intuition of what was baking, for he and ten more Indians decided it was a good time to call on the Wieland home. Not being formal, they entered without knocking, arrayed themselves in squatting position, Indian fashion, along the walls of the room. Mrs. Wieland, after greeting them, passed a bowl of her entire assortment of cookies starting first with Beargrease. Thinking they were all for him he emptied the entire contents into his blanket that he had arranged across his knees and handed back the empty dish. Following Beargrease, the Indians all tracked out. Mrs. Wieland was in tears, for her entire supply of Christmas cookies was gone.[18]

Poor Rosine. But in Anishinabe culture, her magnanimous gift to the chief was completely appropriate. The Anishinabe are a generous people, extravagant givers, lavishing abundantly upon their guests. Presenting the chief with such a gift was only an appropriate gesture of respect for a man of his station. The conventional protocol would then demand that the chief share the goods with his companions. In his observations on the Lake Superior Ojibwe, Johann Kohl, author of *Kitchi-Gami: Life Among the Lake Superior Ojibway*, explains the protocol, stating that according to the unwritten, moral laws of the people, a man was obligated to share all things in common with those who are in want. A person who refused to do so was not respected. Those in positions of leadership, such as Chief Beargrease, bestowed all of their gains upon their followers. Kohl says that the chiefs "give to the tribe not only what they obtain by the chase, but also all the presents they get from the Europeans, even their tribute money."[19] When a chief received gifts or tribute, he would place it all before his followers and invite them to divide it among themselves, sometimes even tossing in his own shirt as a demonstration that he was holding nothing back.

So it was that the Wieland family unwittingly bestowed an appropriate gift upon the chief that he would have, in turn, distributed among the ten men that accompanied him. Whether Chief Moquabimetem went so far as to give them his shirt as well, we do not know, but, at least in the summer months, the chief went about with bare chest, wrapped only in a blanket. Perhaps that is why Edward Greve, author of the unpublished manuscript *The Development of Lake County, MN*, refers to Chief Bear-grease as a "blanket Indian." Greve goes on to report that the chief covered himself in colder months with "clothes of deer buckskin and moccasins of moose hides."[20]

The Chief's Bonnets

In another of Rosine Wieland's generous gestures toward the chief that went awry, she gave him some of her own bonnets. She intended for him to adorn his wives with the bonnets, but Chief Beargrease deemed the colorful headdresses more appropriate for a man of stature than for a woman. He kept them himself. Thereafter the noble Chief Moquabime-tem went about bare-chested, wrapped in a blanket at the waste, moose-hide moccasins on his feet and a colorful bonnet over his long black hair.

Moquabimetem presided over the Indian community at Beaver Bay. A chief in Ojibwe society, however, did not hold absolute power, and different leaders within the community had to be consulted regarding various situations. The decision-making process of an Ojibwe community was decidedly democratic. No one, not even the chiefs, commanded absolute authority. Instead, the chiefs tended to sway decisions by means of their persuasion and influence. A chief offered counsel, not orders. His community looked to him for guidance out of a sense of respect rather than fear.

The Beargrease Family

Chief Beargrease had at least nine children living with him and his two wives in Beaver Bay, and records exist of at least four others. The 1875 State Census of Beaver Bay lists the names and approximate ages of eight of them—the list contains five daughters and three sons. The names and ages of the sons as of the 1875 Census are as follows:

Bebease (15)

Eshquabi (11)

Daiebash (7)

Daiebash (sometimes spelled Daybash or Tay-Baush) is better known by his English name, Peter Beargrease. The eldest son, Bebease, is never further mentioned in any available records. He must have either died or left Beaver Bay shortly after 1875. In either case, his disappearance left Eshquabi, the next eldest, as the heir apparent to the chiefdom. Eshquabi would come to be known by the English name John Beargrease.

Inexplicably, a well-known fourth son is missing from the census report. Skowegan Beargrease was born sometime between 1865 and 1871. He would have been at least four years old when the 1875 census was taken.[21] Skowegan's English name was Joseph Beargrease. He remained unmarried and lived on the North Shore his entire life.

In 1876, the chief took yet another wife (Nabedibejick), and she bore him Gageget Jumuson and another daughter, Esquesinic.

The following table attempts to list the chief's children according to their birth order.[22] The birth years are typically only approximations. The spellings of the names are only faltering attempts at phonetic equivalence by nineteenth-century census agents.

Birth Order	Name	Gender	Birth	Death
1	Otabitowigabonig	Female	1858	
2	Bebease	Male	1860	
3	Newigigikog	Female	1860	
4	Siwanabig	Female	1861	
5	Eshquabi (John)	Male	1862	1910
6	Nawagigibog	Female	1862	
7	Ogimawaskamig	Female	1866	
8	Skowegan (Joseph)	Male	1867	
10	Daybosh (Peter)	Male	1868	1918
12	Gageget Jumuson	Male	1876	
13	Esquesinic	Female	1880	

Inside the Wigwam

During Chief Beargrease's early years at Beaver Bay, he housed his family in a traditional wigwam on the point.[23] Eshquabi's boyhood memories included scenes of domestic life inside that wigwam: his mother preparing a meal, he and his sisters playing quietly nearby, his other mother tending to her own, his father speaking in low tones with men of the clan, and always the sound of Lake Superior's waves gently washing the shore.

One might suppose that the thin walls of the wigwam would prove inadequate in the subzero winter nights which lock down the North Shore in winter months, but Clem Beargrease, the son of Moquabimetem's nephew Mike, testified otherwise. Clem grew up in a wigwam. He told of how they would bend cedar branches to form a frame and wrap it with birchbark. He claimed that the birchbark did not leak, and with a fire in the middle, "it could be forty degrees below zero outside but it was nice and warm inside."[24] Before sleeping at night, the family would heat rocks in the fire and then wrap the rocks in their blankets to keep them warm through the night.

John's Apprenticeship

When Chief Beargrease found local work as a sailor on the schooner *Charley*, young Eshquabi Beargrease accompanied his father on some of those voyages, learning the perilous art of navigating Lake Superior's tempestuous waters. Like his father, Eshquabi eventually took a job as a crewman onboard. In later years, the local papers referred to John Beargrease as "the famous pilot of Beaver Bay."[25] He earned that fame in the mail boat, but Minnesota Historical Society's Anna Anderhagen writes that "when Beargrease was in his late teens, he worked on commercial fishing, passenger, and freight ships that sailed on Lake Superior, including the Schooner, *Charley*."[26]

Chief Beargrease also found work shuttling the mail up and down the shore of Lake Superior. Albert Wieland, the captain of the *Charley*, happened to be the Beaver Bay postmaster and the contract holder for the entire North Shore mail route. He subcontracted the arduous mail route to men of the community, and Chief Beargrease carried the mail frequently on his behalf. So long as the lake was cooperative, the chief took the mail from Superior to Grand Portage by way of rowboat. In the frozen winter months, he packed the mail or relied on a dog team. Young Eshquabi certainly accompanied his father on some of those early mail runs.

Eshquabi's true apprenticeship to his father the chief, however, did not take place on the schooner *Charley* or in the mail boat or behind the dog team. His true apprenticeship was in the way of the woods, the deer, the moose, the caribou, the bear, the trail and the stream, tracking and hunting, setting traps and stretching pelts, trading and bartering, fishing and canoeing. He learned the language and lore of all things, of medicine and spirits, benevolent and otherwise—the ways of his people.

Migrations

Chief Beargrease provided for his family primarily by traditional methods. His daughter, Mrs. Bluesky, described her father's occupation as "trapping and hunting,"[27] which is to say that he lived the life inherited from his fathers before him. In the traditional mode of Ojibwe life, trapping and hunting formed part of the regular, migratory pattern. Families tended to visit and annually revisit the same summer hunting grounds, and hunting lands were passed from father to son.

March thaws caused the maple sap to run, and the women and children set out for the sugar bush camps. In those days, a stand of maple trees stretched parallel to Lake Superior north of Grand Marais. This was the primary sugar bush for the North Shore Anishinabe. The annual migration to the sugar bush was such a regular rhythm of life in Beaver Bay that the road north to the camps was called "The Sugar Bush Trail." Davis reports that the Sugar Bush Trail left the Beaver Bay "Town Road" to climb over the hills east of Beaver Bay at the intersection where today stands the Silver Bay traffic light on Highway 61.[28]

All the Ojibwe families of Beaver Bay participated in the annual excursion to the sugar bush. Sugar bushing was a woman's vocation, but while the women tapped trees, gathered fire wood and boiled maple sap into sugar, the men hunted. Helen Wieland Skillings describes the Beaver Bay Indians leaving for the sugar camps every spring and then returning a month later, considerably plumper, the children with "faces as round as the moon and polished like shiny apples" from the steady diet of sugar they had consumed over the preceding weeks.[29] The settlers anticipated their return, eager to trade for the sweet sugars and syrup.

Summers were given to hunting and fishing. The deer, moose, bear and vanishing caribou were staples. Lake Superior teemed with trout, sturgeon, pike, black bass, herring, whitefish and a variety of other species. In the early autumn, it was time to set out for inland lakes to harvest the wild rice and store up winter provisions. The winter months always meant hardship, but inland lakes and streams provided ice fishing and trapping opportunities. Chief Moquabimetem's work on the schooner *Charley* and income from the mail run were only secondary to these primary means of survival. The frequent migrations meant long absences from the Beaver Bay community which likely explains the occasional gaps in census records where Beargrease names vanish in a particular year, only to reappear later.

Christianity and the Medicine Dance

The religion of the Beaver Bay Indian community was a conglomeration of Christianity and traditional Anishinabe medicine ways. The

Christianization of the community began early. In 1874, Reverend John Lueder came to teach school and religion in Beaver Bay. He was the first clergyman to take up residence in town. Since Beaver Bay did not yet have a church, Reverend Lueder conducted services in the schoolhouse.

> [Reverend Lueder was] astonished to see several Indians dressed in their blankets and feathers seated among the worshippers at one of his early church services in Beaver Bay. He was a little apprehensive, but noticing that the members of the congregation seemed to take it as a matter of course, he continued bravely with his sermon. The Indians seemed to be listening with close attention. At the close of the service, he approached a befeathered brave and asked him in German if he had understood what had been spoken. Reverend Lueder was abashed when in perfect German the old brave answered, "Of course I understood everything, for you spoke very distinctly."[30]

In addition to Reverend Lueder's sermons, the famous Catholic missionary-priest, Bishop Frederic Baraga, frequently stopped at Beaver Bay on his journeys along the shore. Baraga was known in the woods as "the snowshoe priest." When in Beaver Bay, he stayed several days as the honored guest of Henry and Rosine Wieland. Bishop Baraga is remembered for his tireless efforts in improving the standard of living for Lake Superior Ojibwe, defending their rights against white encroachment, ministering to their medical needs and converting them to Catholicism. His greatest contribution to Anishinabe culture was his work in the Ojibwe language. As a necessary part of his missionary efforts, he created the first dictionary of the Ojibwe language and translated parts of the Bible and a Catholic prayer book into Ojibwe. On one occasion, he gave a copy of his dictionary to Rosine. He hoped that a few language skills might help her to better cope with life among the Beaver Bay Indians.

Every place that Bishop Baraga went, he conducted baptisms. The Beaver Bay Indian community, like most North Shore Anishinabe, was soon converted to Catholicism.

Despite the best of missionary efforts, however, the Beargrease family never abandoned the old ways. Whites regarded John Beargrease as a medicine man, and he still practiced traditional medicine rituals to the end of his life.[31]

The Two Harbors Iron News once reported on John Beargrease's work as the mail carrier and also commented, "John is one of the Indians who don't bother with the ghost dance…"[32] But in reality, he did. The Beaver

Bay Ojibwe held regular medicine dances on the gravel peninsula separating the Beaver River from the bay. These practices made the white settlers uneasy, but they never tried to hamper the rites. It is amusing to see the ritual dance through the eyes of the wary, white neighbors:

> The din and noise of the Indian drums and the dancing and singing during this ritual drove some of the settlers nearly to distraction, for this would continue for days. Their song was something like this: wa ha jaw a ha ha wa nee ha ha, and was accompanied by rhythms beaten on their skin-covered drums, measuring 18 to 20 inches in diameter and 4 or 5 inches in depth.[33]

Though his household continued in the old ways, Moquabimetem's children regarded themselves as Catholic. Catholic or not, Eshquabi Beargrease grew up immersed in the traditional ways of his people, and he never abandoned them.

Letter from Beaver Bay

The archives at the Bois Forte Heritage Center preserve an 1883 handwritten letter from the Beargrease family at Beaver Bay inquiring about the timing of annuity payments.[34] The letter implies that several of the Indians of Beaver Bay had an interest in the annuities paid at Lake Vermillion. One of the settlers must have written it for Chief Beargrease, or possibly on behalf of his son John. Neither John nor his father were literate, nor were any of John's siblings. The letter provides certain evidence of a connection between the Beaver Bay Beargrease family and the Nett Lake Beargrease family.

Beaver Bay, Minn.
Dec 13/83

Dear Sir,
The Indians in the neighborhood would like to know from you at what time about, the payment at Vermillion will come off please drop a card stating about the time within a week or so befor (sic) the time that payment will be at Vermillion Lake and very much oblige.
Beargrease Indian at Beaver Bay, Lake Co. Minn.

The Passing of the Chief

As the years at Beaver Bay passed, the chief's children grew and married. The 1885 State Census is the last record of Chief Beargrease. He appears on the census still living in Beaver Bay with his two wives: Bid-owadeganan (probably the same as Bidwivegamibag) and Eshegamigan. His teenage son Daybosh (Peter) is the last child at home. The census esti-mated the chief's age to be fifty-five, his wives around fifty, and Daybosh is listed as sixteen. Living in another dwelling at least nine houses away was another wife, a thirty-six-year-old woman with the Beargrease sur-name, a young wife named Nabedibejick. She appears to have been living alone with her two children: her son Gageget Jumuson and her daughter Esquesinic.

No records tell us specifically when the chief died, but it must have happened sometime shortly after that 1885 census. According to his son Peter, the chief died of pneumonia.[35] The Beaver Bay Indian community that had previously looked to the chief for leadership now looked to his oldest son Eshquabi, so John Beargrease became the default patriarch of the Beargrease clan and the chief of Beaver Bay.

CHAPTER THREE

Celerity, Certainty and Security

John Beargrease was not the first North Shore mailman.

In the mid-nineteenth century, Congress passed an act which allowed the postmaster general to award mail-carrying contracts to the lowest bidder, so long as the bidder would provide for the due celerity, certainty and security of such transportation. The mail service referred to such bids for carrying the mail as "celerity, certainty and security bids." When preparing documents, postal clerks abbreviated the cumbersome term by substituting it with three asterisks or stars (*** bids). The convention was so common that postal workers began to refer to contract routes as "star routes." The post office let the coveted star route contracts to the lowest bidder.

It was the era of stagecoach mail carriers, the Pony Express and mail-by-rail. As settlers spread out to ever further and more remote locations, the Postal Service relied more and more upon the star route contractors to deliver the mail.

In an age of instant communication, it is difficult for us to understand the vital role that such mail service played in the communities of the early North Shore settlers. The rugged miles of Lake Superior's wild shoreline effectively cut the pioneers off from the outside world. Flanked on one side by endless miles of uninhabited, barely passable wilderness and on the other by the unforgiving, treacherous waters of Lake Superior, the North Shore settlers struggled to maintain links with civilization. The mail service, therefore, represented their only reliable communication with the outside world. In the summer months, the isolation was felt less acutely. Steamers, sailboats and even rowboats bearing passengers, goods, periodicals and personal mail allowed them at least weekly contact with the rest of the world. A shopping trip from Grand Marais to Duluth and back was possible. In the winter, however, when the waters became non-navigable and the ports at Superior and Duluth were locked in ice jams, the North Shore settlers found themselves utterly alone. Their sense of isolation in the midst of that numbing cold was acute. The only way to reach the rest of the world was to commit to a hazardous journey by rowboat or a long, wearisome trek by snowshoe. The settlers regarded the mail carriers who dared to battle the extreme rigors of the perilous route as heroes. Without the monthly or weekly mail that they brought, the settlers found themselves consigned to long, lonely months of total isolation from the outside world.

And the mail carrier carried more than mail. He carried the news from up and down the shore. ("Down the shore" was the direction northeast toward Grand Portage and Canada. "Up the shore" meant the direction southwest toward Superior and Duluth.) The mail carrier was the weekly source of gossip and information about neighbors and friends. When his dogsled pulled into town, he was quickly surrounded by settlers, eager to hear the latest: glad news of a wedding or a birth, word of new settlers, a sad story about a tragedy, rumors about prospecting, shocking tales about scandals and controversies, local politics, illness and plague, the sad news of a death, a funeral, the chilling tale of a shipwreck or a fisherman lost on the lake. The mail carrier carried all of this, connecting the isolated settlers with one another and the outside world.

McLean and the First North Shore Mail Route

In July of 1856, two years before the first Anishinabe settled in Beaver Bay and six years before John Beargrease was born, the Postal Service initiated a star route connecting Superior, Wisconsin with Grand Portage. Thomas Clark of Beaver Bay landed the mail contract. He hired his former employee and future son-in-law, "little Bob" McLean, to make the arduous journey between Grand Portage and Duluth and back. In his *Reminiscences*, R. B. McLean writes, "I had the honor of taking the first mail through on the route." McLean was already serving as the postmaster at Beaver Bay, and apparently courting Clark's daughter; the two were later married.

The mail arrived in Superior by way of steamers from the east or on the backs of packers who carried it up from Saint Paul. In later years, a stage line opened between Saint Paul and Superior. From Superior, the mail route north followed the shoreline as far as Grand Portage.

McLean first ran the mail by way of a Mackinaw rowboat. As late as 1876, he was delivering the mail "using an 18-foot cedar rowboat equipped with sails."[1]

In most years, the lake is open for navigation from May to December. The weather, of course, is unpredictable, and Lake Superior is renowned for her violent mood swings, but on many fine summer days, the surface of the Lake shows barely a ripple. Mail carriers like R. B. McLean (and in later years, John Beargrease) loaded mail sacks made of waterproof canvas or hides into the bottom of their boats and set out, using a combination of oars and sails while they hugged the coast up and down the route. When the weather was agreeable, the mail carrier would stay at the oars day and night to try to complete the route before winds, rain and treacherous waves arose.

That first North Shore mail route went monthly from Superior to Grand Portage with a stop in Beaver Bay and a few other communities along the way.[2] According to Otto Wieland, it took two weeks round-trip. "Quite a long time to wait for your daily paper or a love letter," he observed.[3]

Little Bob McLean would have found ports-of-call to be few and far between. After Beaver Bay, he did not encounter another post office until the faltering little settlement at Grand Marais, another fifty-seven miles down the shore. Within two years, the settlers at Grand Marais abandoned their claims, and the post office was closed. Thirteen years would pass before the mail was delivered to Grand Marais again.

McLean would have left Grand Marais for Grand Portage, forty miles further down the shore. Grand Portage is named for the nine-mile portage the voyageurs used to make around the impassable waterfalls and rapids of the Pigeon River as they canoed bales of pelts down from Canada. During the height of the fur trade, Grand Portage was the site of the great rendezvous and became headquarters for various fur trading enterprises.

By the days of R. B. McLean, however, the fur trade had all but vanished from Grand Portage. A small trading post maintained by H. H. McCullough and his employee Henry Elliot doubled as a post office at Grand Portage.

From Grand Portage, McLean took the mail to fishing and copper mining communities on Isle Royale, twenty-two miles off the mainland. After a journey of approximately 170 miles, McLean turned about to return to Grand Portage and sail back up the shore all the way back to Superior.

Aside from Beaver Bay, no substantial settlements stood between Superior and Grand Portage, and Grand Portage itself was scarcely a settlement with only its native Ojibwe population and the McCullough trading post.

As McLean shuttled those first mails up and down the shore of the Lake, he passed by the imaginary, platted towns of Portland, Endion, Belville, Oneota, Clifton, Montezuma, Knife River, Agate Bay, Burlington, Marmata, Encampment, Waterville, Saxton, Valley Field, Rice's Point, Trenton, and a host of others.[4] They were towns in name only, a result of dozens of preemptors and settlers who had staked out claims and submitted plats for future townsites along the shore, but most of them had come to naught. A few of the sites boasted a cabin or two, a settler here, an empty cabin there. In 1856, McLean took note of Fred Ryder's house, "the first house built in the village of Duluth."

The Wieland Years

McLean resigned his commission as Beaver Bay postmaster in November of 1856. The following August, Albert Wieland took over Beaver Bay's post office, and shortly thereafter the Postal Service awarded him the star route contract for the North Shore. On the 1860 Federal Census, Albert listed his occupation as mail contractor. McLean listed his as fisherman. The Wielands retained the contract for most of the ensuing three decades.[5]

Albert Wieland often made the mail trip himself, sometimes with the able assistance of his young nephew Henry (H. P. Wieland). On other occasions, Albert subcontracted the route to McLean[6] and to "reliable Indians" from the Beaver Bay community. John Morrison and Chief Beargrease were among the reliable Indians who carried the mail.[7]

As a young boy in the mid 1870s, Eshquabi Beargrease would have often waited expectantly for his father's boat to round the bay, laden with mail bags. He must have spent many a long, cold winter day straining his ears for the sound of his father's dog-team bells to come drifting through the quiet, frozen woods. On some occasions, young Eshquabi would have accompanied his father, sitting in the bottom of the boat atop the mail bags, or riding on the dogsled, learning the trail.

Carrying the mail by rowboat on tempestuous Lake Superior was hazardous enough, but mail carriers certainly preferred the difficulties of summer's sudden storms and choppy waters to the rigors of North Shore winters. They learned endurance pulling at the oars with frozen hands while navigating the stormy lake, rowing among the shifting ice floes, pushing their small skiffs over broken ice until dropping back into open water, raising a sail to catch a breath of favorable wind and quickly dropping it when the wind shifted. When the churning, frigid waters of winter no longer allowed for mail by sail, mail carriers resorted to packsack, dogsled and snowshoe.

The overland route was a race with the mail carrier hobbling along on snow shoes behind a dog-team and toboggan. They traveled over the most unforgiving of trails, blocked by wind falls, cutting across the ice of half frozen rivers, risking shortcuts across frozen bays on the lake, finding themselves caught in sudden avalanche-like blizzards. In an article entitled "U.S. Mail on the North Shore," Otto Wieland described the hazards of the mail route, the shifting ice on Lake Superior, the sudden storms and all the difficulties of land and sea. "It does not require a lively imagination to appreciate the fact that these early mail carriers were exposed to many dangers and vicissitudes, both in winter and in summer," he wrote.[8]

Mary Emmons (Parker) related some anecdotes about mail carriers from that era. She lived with her pioneer family at the mouth of the Pigeon River. In the 1860s, the Parkers operated a modest trading post there in the midst of the Grand Portage Ojibwe community. They had a large, comfortable home surrounded by several log buildings which housed the Indians they employed. Mary Emmons recalled the arrival of the monthly mail:

> The winters were very severe and we were practically isolated. As I remember about once a month the mail would arrive on dog sleighs or toboggans from Fort William, and I remember one incident when the mail came in [with] one of the party having frozen feet and my father had to amputate several of his toes. Another time the mail carrier came from Fort William, they brought scarlet fever to our household and several of the family, myself included were very ill with it for many weeks.[9]

H. P. Wieland's Memories

During the early years of the Wieland mail route, young H. P. Wieland, the son of Henry and Rosine, often accompanied his uncle Albert and the other mail carriers on their monthly trips. "I did enjoy those days. It was real life. None of your hustle and bustle of the present days," Wieland recollected.[10]

He claimed that it took ten to fifteen days to make a round-trip from

Superior to Grand Portage by rowboat. Whenever the wind was favorable they would raise the sail, but most of the time they had to row. If the waves on the lake became too formidable, he and the other mail carrier would pull ashore and wait out the storm. If it rained, they would tip the boat over and crawl under it for shelter until the rain subsided.

He often carried the mail with John Morrison, one of the Beaver Bay Indians. On one occasion, after a long day at the oars, he and Morrison landed on a little beach near Stewart River about 1 A.M. No sooner had they settled down to sleep a few hours than they were visited by a polecat—a skunk. Wieland describes laying breathlessly on the beach while the skunk sniffed around their faces and belongings. When the skunk finally ambled off into the brush, Morrison jumped to his feet and threw a rock into the bushes where the skunk had disappeared. Wieland says, "She didn't come back, but two very tired mail carriers found it necessary to break camp as quickly as possible, to get their boat launched and to hurry away in search of some other fresh air hostelry."[11]

On one mail boat trip, Henry Wieland and his uncle Albert had a close encounter with a shooting star:

> On one of these trips, in the latter part of October, 1868, my uncle and I were returning from Grand Portage to Duluth. It was a very dark night. About midnight, just after we had passed the mouth of the Temperance River, a very bright star suddenly appeared in the northeastern sky.
>
> It proved to be a meteor, for it increased very rapidly in size and brightness, and for a few seconds it seemed to be coming straight toward our boat at a terrific speed. Both of us were frightened almost out of our wits, and the illumination was so dazzling that we were blinded for several minutes. With a terrible roar it passed us, apparently about three quarters of a mile inland, and struck the ground with a deafening crash some distance ahead of us.
>
> When we were again able to see, we continued on our way; for a considerable time neither of us spoke a word.[12]

The mailbags were light in that first decade of North Shore mail service. As Albert Wieland and his Beaver Bay mail contractors traversed the distance up and down the shore, they used the occasion for trading with trappers and Indians along the route. They packed the mail boat or dogsled with furs collected along the way and sold them to dealers in Superior for profit.[13] It was not long, however, until the mailbags began to get heavier.

Silver Island

In 1868, prospectors discovered a major silver lode in a tiny rock island. The island, shaped like a human skull protruding from the water, was a sacred place to the Anishinabe. After 1868, it became sacred to the white people, too. The Silver Islet mining operation quickly grew into a major enterprise employing nearly 1,000 men. In the summer months, steamers handled the mail service to Silver Islet. By 1871 a steamer was carrying the mail out of Duluth every Thursday with stops in Beaver Bay, Silver Islet and Fort William.[14] In the winter months, however, mail service back and forth along the shore again fell to the rowboat or overland travel. In 1884, the mining operation's pumps failed when a coal shipment did not arrive on time. Lake Superior's waters quickly reclaimed the deep shafts of Silver Islet, forcing an end to the enterprise. The mine was never reopened.

Grand Marais

The early years of the 1870s saw new settlers arriving at Grand Marais. Prospector and land speculator Ed Wakelin and his friend, the intrepid entrepreneur, explorer, prospector and speculator Henry Mayhew, purchased the abandoned claims along Grand Marais' double harbor. The fur trader Sam Howenstine, a former employee of the McCullough fur operation, joined them. Mayhew, Wakelin and Howenstine secured all the land left behind by the original Grand Marais settlers, as well as the valuable land along both bays.[15] The new Grand Marais pioneers and the tiny community that formed around them soon needed mail service.

In 1873, Henry Mayhew applied with the U.S. Postal Service to reopen the Grand Marais post office. He received the appointment of postmaster, a position he retained for the next twenty years. The Grand Marais post office operated out of a two-story building owned by Mayhew. The same building also functioned as trading post, schoolhouse, county courthouse, doctor's office and town-center.

Early Star Route Men

Vickie Chupurdia, a keeper of Beargrease lore, reported that John Beargrease first began running the mail in 1879.[16] He was in his early twenties. He still worked on the schooner *Charley* during the navigational season. Carrying the mail during the winter months supplemented his income. Albert Wieland, the schooner's first captain, still held the rights to the star route contract. John Beargrease was only one of several subcontractors who Albert hired to carry the weekly mail from Duluth/Superior to Grand Marais.

Sam Howenstine of Grand Marais put in a stint on the star route mail service. For two winters in the 1870s Sam had four men working for him and three dog teams pulling 400 to 700 pounds of mail on toboggans.[17] The high volume of mail was bound for Silver Island. During the 1880s, Howenstine occasionally carried the mail on the shorter route between Grand Marais and Grand Portage. Thus Howenstine joined the ever growing ranks of North Shore mail carriers like R. B. McLean, Albert Wieland, John Morrison and Chief Beargrease.

Other names deserve mention as well. The February 3, 1872 edition of the *Duluth Minnesotan* described a mail carrier named J. W. Owen who carried the mail "per trail and snow shoes." Willis Raff wrote of a mail carrier named George Ward who used four dogs and a toboggan to deliver the mail one winter in the 1880s before becoming a lighthouse keeper and then a ship's captain.[18] For a short period of time, Joseph Betzler, an outstanding Beaver Bay pioneer and a good friend of the Beargrease family, was carrying the mail twice a month. Betzler carried the mail from Duluth to Beaver Bay, and Beargrease carried it from Beaver Bay to Grand Marais and back. Betzler needed the extra income to help feed his ever-growing family. He fathered twenty-one children by the same woman, thereby becoming a literal patriarch to a significant portion of Beaver Bay's population.

On the other end of the mail route, another Joseph was carrying the mail. Joseph Godfrey Montferrand was a prominent Grand Marais citizen and registered member of the Grand Portage band of Ojibwe. Montferrand worked the route from Grand Marais to Grand Portage. While delivering the mail, Montferrand sometimes brought along his nephew, the young teenager, Louis E. M. Plante.

Louis Plante, in turn, became a famous mail musher in his own right. He worked in relay with Beargrease, the latter carrying the mail as far down the shore as Grand Marais and the former carrying it on from Grand Marais to Grand Portage. Plante's reputation as a North Shore mail carrier is rivaled only by that of John Beargrease. Plante earned $24.00 a month carrying weekly mails between Grand Marais and Grand Portage. He claimed that he "wore out a pair of moccasins on each trip."[19]

CHAPTER FOUR

John and Louise

The early settlers of the North Shore recalled John Beargrease in vivid detail. In *The Development of Lake County, MN*, Edward Greve describes Beargrease as "thin, rawboned, strong, sinewy, wiry, and well built about five feet ten inches in height. He was usually quiet, spoke poor English, and had long black hair." Another local history collection recalls, "He was not the typical Ojibway as photos and accounts describe them, but an unusually tall man, lean and with a determined stride, a bearing which suggested mixed blood not alien to this area at that time."[1] Yet another reminiscence claims that "John's eyes bore an unyielding fierceness and that his comportment as a cunning loner was typical of the woodsman…"[2] No sooner had this young, wiry teenager with fierce, unyielding eyes and determined stride begun his first mail runs than he found himself in love with a local Beaver Bay girl.

The Wishcop Family

La Louise Wishcop was the daughter of a prominent Beaver Bay Anishinabe family. Her mother was a three-quarter blood Ojibwe woman named Marianne Devaux who originally came from Grand Portage. When Marianne was about sixteen years old, she married the full blooded Joseph Wischop. Historical documents are particularly ambiguous about the spelling of Wishcop: Wishcob, Wishcoob, Wishcoop, Wishgob, Wishcomb, Wisbob, Weescob, to name a few of the variations.

Marianne bore three children to Wischop while they lived in Grand

Portage: Nelson (who was also called Ole) in 1858, Cecile in 1859 and La Louise in 1864. Shortly after the birth of Louise, the family relocated to the growing Ojibwe community in Beaver Bay.[3] While at Beaver Bay, Joseph and Marianne had two more sons: Narcis (who was also known as Lasis) and Joseph Jr. Only a few years later, Joseph Sr. died leaving Marianne as a widow with five young children.

Alex Boyer, a half-blood of French Canadian descent and a recent widower himself, married Marianne and took in her family. Alex was better known in Beaver Bay by the nickname of "Giggity" because of his expressive use of that word in place of profanity.[4] Marianne took the last name Boyer rather than Giggity, but her children retained their natural father's name of Wishcop. The Wishcop daughters are important to the Beargrease story because both of them became Beargrease brides.

In Ojibwe culture, young girls were closely guarded, especially as suitors began to come calling. The girls were taught to be modest and circumspect. If a young man wished to visit a girl, he might do so only under careful supervision. He had to pay due respect to the parents and, if he wanted to impress them, would bring in a deer or other trophy of the hunt as a gift. One common custom was for young men to play melodies on a special courting flute outside the girl's home in the evenings, but play as he might, the girl was never allowed to be lured out by him.[5]

Beargrease married the young, pretty Louise in late 1880.[6] Louise was sixteen years old, and her groom John Beargrease was nineteen. Ordinarily, a girl remained at home for a short while after her marriage. The young couple would integrate into the family until they were prepared to start their own home. Almost immediately, the new family suffered a setback. Any work Beargrease had on the schooner *Charley* ended abruptly that May when the ship was washed aground at Beaver Bay. The mail route became his main source of income.

Antone

On July 27, 1881, John and Louise's first child was born to them. If Beargrease chose to name his children according to traditional Anishinabe custom, the child remained nameless until the father (or a designated namer) had the right dream. The child was then named after an object or element that appeared in the dream.[7] In addition to an Ojibwe name, Beargrease gave each child an English name. History has recorded only a few of the Ojibwe names of Beargrease's children. Beargrease gave his first son the white name Antone.

Antone lived only one month. In accordance with the ways of her people, Louise would have followed certain rites concerning the death of her son. An Anishinabe mother bereaved of an infant child kept a lock of her baby's hair wrapped in precious adornment, such as paper and ribbons, along with a few personal effects. Over the course of a year, the mother kept the memento ever near her, treating it almost like a doll, even as she would have nurtured her infant. At the end of twelve months, she unbundled the lock of hair and burned it, finally letting go of grief and entrusting her child to the next world.

Another old Ojibwe custom encouraged relocation after the death of a family member—at least temporarily. After the death of Antone, Louise's parents left Beaver Bay and relocated in Grand Marais. John and Louise left with them.

In 1882, the government undertook a massive harbor project at Grand Marais. So many Ojibwe people moved to Grand Marais looking for work that they formed a small Indian suburb on the eastern end of the town called Chippewa City. The Boyers moved to Chippewa City as a part of that migration. Beargrease might have found work as a laborer on the harbor construction project as well.

Janet and Charlotte

While living in Grand Marais with her parents, Louise gave birth to a daughter whom they named Janet. Two years later, a second daughter named Charlotte came, but Louise's joy over the birth of baby Charlotte was dampened by another sorrow. On April 15, 1885, the State Census found John, Louise and two-year-old Janet living in the home of Louise's father Alex Boyer in Grand Marais. Seven weeks later, on June 8, 1885, Beaver Bay pioneer Jacob Hangartner recorded the census information for his village. He listed John and Louise living with their infant daughter Charlotte in a home in Beaver Bay, but no Janet, meaning that during those intervening seven weeks, Janet had died. Just as they had done after the death of Antone, John and Louise relocated. The harbor work in Grand Marais was complete, and there was no reason to remain, so the family returned to Beaver Bay.

The Beargrease Home

Back in Beaver Bay, John and Louise rented a house of their own. Popular local legends want to place Beargrease and his family in a Beaver Bay wigwam. Though he lived in one of the wigwams on the Beaver Bay point as a boy, there is no indication that he did so as an adult. On the contrary, the young family made their home in one of the many hewn wood houses readily available for rent.[8] The 1900 Federal Census schedule entitled *Special Inquiries Relating to Indians* indicates that, at least by then, all the Indians of Beaver Bay were residing in permanent homes. Earlier census lists did not make those types of distinctions, but Beaver Bay certainly had plenty of vacant cabins available for rent. The 1860 Federal Census lists dozens of unoccupied homes in the Beaver Bay vicinity, homes left behind by disillusioned settlers who left during the financial panic of 1857.

Even though they did not live in a wigwam, the John Beargrease home was a traditional Anishinabe home. Such a home did not contain much in the way of furniture. The typical family took their meals on the floor, sat on the floor and slept on the floor. Mary Lornston-Hangartner, a friend of the Beargrease daughters and frequent visitor to the Beargrease home, recalled "the peculiar but not unpleasant odor of tanned deer hide pervaded all the Indian homes."[9] And, of course, there were the dogs. Dogs were common to Ojibwe homes, and they took a share in most of the family life. John's dogs were family members.

Handicrafts

John Beargrease and his wife possessed the traditional skills inherited from their culture. Aside from raising children, Louise made herself busy with the chores common to the Indian wife. Her clever fingers worked skillfully in fabrics, leather, beads and birchbark. The Beargrease home produced clothing, moccasins and snowshoes, all made in the traditional manner:

> Mary [Lornston] Hangartner tells how, in later years, she and Augusta Beargrease made doll clothes at the Beargrease home, from scraps of bright cloth which old John would bring from Two Harbors, probably for his daughter Charlotte who did sewing for some of the Indian families.[10]

One of the traditional handicrafts common to Ojibwe women was the construction of the *tikinagan*. The *tikinagan* functioned as a sort of

cradle and baby carrier. The Ojibwe mother began with a flat piece of poplar board to which she attached a small frame of thin, peeled wood. She
fashioned the frame to fit the shape of the child's body snugly. She tied
it on with bast cords, and then stuffed the snug compartment with a soft
mixture of fine dry moss, spongy cedar chips and milkweed cotton. In this
cozy bed, the baby was bound and snuggled up to the armpits. Over the
babies head, she fastened a stiff arch of wood to protect the child. Should
the *tikinagan* ever fall over, it came to rest on the wooden arch rather than
the baby's head. When bundled inside, the baby was safe from most of the
normal buffets and jostles life had to offer. After completing the *tikinagan*,
the Ojibwe mother then decorated it with toys: a pair of small moccasins,
a tiny bow, a wooden ring, a round piece of caribou leather, all dangling in
reach of the child. As a final touch, she covered over the entire apparatus
with brightly colored cloth.[11]

More Daughters and Sons

Beargrease and his wife remained in Beaver Bay for the rest of his life
and went on to fill many *tikinagan's*. In all, Louise birthed ten more children. The sources listing births and names of the Beargrease children contain numerous discrepancies, particularly in regard to birth years, but the
following approximations cannot be too far removed from the actual fact.

In 1885, shortly after their return to Beaver Bay, Louise bore a third
daughter. They gave her the English name Mary Ann, naming her after
Louise's mother. In March of 1889, a second son, Peter, was born, but
Peter lived only three months. Within a year of Peter's death, Augusta,
their fourth daughter, was born. Some records mistakenly indicate that
Augusta died in early childhood as well. She did not. Confusion regarding Augusta arises because in later years she went by the name Constance.
Both Augusta (Constance) and Mary lived into adulthood and had children of their own.

A Bay Area Historical Society genealogy document of the Beargrease
family lists a son named Ahin (Ahm) born on June 9, 1892, but like his
older brothers, he lived only a short life and died before the age of two.
According to the Grand Portage rolls, in 1894, the same year that Ahin
died, a son named Gwei-we-sens was born to the Beargrease family, but
like his older brothers, he died in infancy. It must have seemed to John and
Louise that fate would not allow them a surviving son.

Then Joseph was born into their family. Joseph proved to be a healthy son. He was followed in birth order by Amabilis (Mabel, May) Louise, a fifth daughter in 1896. The Grand Portage rolls record the birth of John George in October of 1899 and his death a month later.[12] According to the Bay Area Historical Society genealogy, George, the last son, was born on April 1, 1901. The last daughter born to John and Louise was Francis (Nancy) in 1905. If all of these are correct, Beargrease fathered thirteen children.

The following chart lists John and Louise's children. The children's birth years often conflict from one record to another and should be used with caution.

Birth Order	Name	Gender	Birth	Death
1	Antone	Male	7/27/1881	8/27/1881
2	Janet	Female	1883	1884-1885
3	Charlotte	Female	1884-1885	4/4/1908
4	Mary Ann	Female	1885	4/9/1923
5	Augusta (Constance)	Female	1889-1900	7/1912
6	Peter	Male	3/1889	9/1889
7	Ahin (Ahm)	Male	6/9/1892	2/27/1894
8	Gwei-we-sens	Male	1893-1894?	5/1894
9	Joseph	Male	1892 or 6/2/1894	3/7/1911
10	Amabilis (Mabel, May) Louise	Female	11/24/1896	6/13/1915
11	John George	Male	10/1899	11/29/1899
12	George	Male	4/1/1901	12/12/1918
13	Francis (Nancy)	Female	1905	11/7/1956

Family Life

Traditional Anihsinabe parents bestowed doting admiration and tender affection on their children. In the typical family, parents never treated their children with severity, nor did they even raise their voices. Fathers might have been stern but never severe. Corporal punishment was unheard of among Anishinabe families, yet the children were characteristically quiet, orderly and always respectful of parents. A passerby rarely heard the din of wild children issuing from an Indian home. Settlers and Europeans agreed that is impossible to find quieter and more polite children than those of the Ojibwe.

In his observations on nineteenth century Ojibwe domestic life, Kohl speaks of mothers regularly setting aside their work to "look tenderly at their children, run up and kiss them, put their hands, ribbons or caps straight, sit down on the grass for a minute, lost in admiration of the little one."[13] In another passage, he offers a glimpse of an Ojibwe father spending time with his children:

> I knew an Indian hunter, who was a most exemplary and amiable father of a family. When he returned home in the evening from the chase, his squaw had a warm dish in readiness for him. She wrung out his wet clothes and moccasins, and hung them round the fire to dry. After he had supped he would lie down on his bed, and the children would nestle round him. He would joke and play with the little ones, called the elder children to him, questioned them as to their conduct, gave them good lessons and rules of life, and told them stories.[14]

The homecoming would have been no different for John Beargrease. Returning from the mail route after an absence of several days, he finds warm, dry clothing laid ready, food for the dogs, a warm meal for himself and his three eldest daughters eager to surround him and hear a tale of mailman-adventure or a bit of news from the trail. As the little ones drop off to sleep that night, Louise draws the blankets and hides more closely round the children. The black-haired heads and glittering eyes of the older girls peer out from under the woolen blankets and thick furs as they listen to their father's stories.

Provider

In addition to the mail run, Beargrease stayed busy with various vocations. In the old days, the man's role in Ojibwe culture was focused primarily on the glamour of hunting and trapping and occasionally going to war. Aside from bringing home game meat, Anishinabe women carried most of the load of responsibility for the family's well being. The man's job was to provide, and in the old ways, that meant hunting. Following his father's lead, Beargrease adapted his traditional role to the broader scope of the emerging modern world in which he found himself. He poured his energy into the hunt for provision, whether that meant chasing a mail sled across the frozen north or punching ore on the docks of Two Harbors.

Beargrease's diligence and gainful employment brought success for his family. When the daughters grew older, they supplemented the family income by sewing clothes for the local Indian community and working as domestic help. So long as they had the mail route income, the John Beargrease family was better off than the average Beaver Bay Indian family. By modern standards, that is still desperately poor, but by the standards of the day, they were doing tolerably well.

A family photo taken sometime around 1895 testifies to their relative affluence. It depicts John and Louise with four children. John is dressed in a handsome suit and tie with a bowler hat. Louise, looking possibly pregnant (perhaps with Mabel?) is stylishly dressed in a Sunday hat, scarf and button-down dress, with a traditionally plaited blanket over her shoulders as a shawl. Augusta, Charlotte and Mary are smartly dressed in what could only have been their finest and most expensive clothes: matching broad-collared, button-down dresses, neckerchiefs and sombrero-like Sunday hats complete with ribbons. Little Joseph is decked out in similar finery, seated on his father's lap, giving the camera a suspicious and distrustful look. New clothes in honor of an Easter service likely occasioned the photograph. It is the only surviving photograph of Beargrease with his family.

Though both Beargrease and his wife Louise were illiterate, they insisted on education for their children. A 1905 Beaver Bay school photo printed in *Beaver Bay, Original North Shore Village* depicts Mabel and Joseph Beargrease posing with the other school children in front of the old one-room schoolhouse.[15] The census records report all of the Beargrease children enrolled in school.

Beargrease and the Grog

Once a year, Beargrease made an annual January pilgrimage back to the Bois Forte / Nett Lake reservation to collect his tribal annuity payment. An 1886 document on United States Indian Service letterhead issued from the La Pointe Agency at Vermillion Lake, Minnesota, now in the Bois Forte archives, provides evidence of this. It also provides evidence for his preference for alcohol:[16]

United States Indian Service,
La Pointe Agency
V. Lake Minn. Jan[uar]y 16, 1886.
J. T. Gregory Eag.
U.S. Ind. Agt.
Ashland, Wis.

Sir,

Here is two cases of selling whiskey to Indians, and is a sure go if parties are arrested. Jan[uary] 14th, 1886, Rob[er]t McKay sold whiskey to John Robinson, an Indian that drew pay the last payment, Jan[uar]y 15th 1886 sold whiskey to John Beargrease an Indian belonging to this tribe also Wa sha wa gi jig and A scwe gi jig.

Can get as many witnesses as are required. And if it is attended to at once, all the parties could be found here. Hope this will be attended too. This Rob't McKay is the fellow who was in St. Paul all summer.

Very Respectfully
[Signature Illegible]
Teacher

In those times, local laws often made it illegal to sell alcohol to Indians. Apparently, Beargrease used a portion of the annuity to purchase some whiskey. Despite the rigid temperance laws, purveyors of alcohol commonly made such transactions, particularly after the January annuity payments. The annuity payment was well understood as an annual celebration by both Indians and settlers, and such a celebration requires at least a modicum of cheer. It is unlikely that the case was ever prosecuted.

Beargrease found it necessary to celebrate regularly throughout the year though. Early pioneer recollections of John Beargrease often observe his affection for alcohol. Like many of his contemporary North Shoremen, Beargrease was a fairly regular and heavy drinker. At least one drinking bout landed him in jail for a few days, but it would be unfair to characterize him as a drunk. Those who remember his drinking also point out that he never let the alcohol take control. William Stein of Two Harbors recalled that John "could be merry if the grog were plentiful. More than once … he was poured into a rowboat laden with mail and pointed toward the deep water of Lake Superior where he immediately became a professional."[17] His drinking never impeded his competence as a mail carrier—well, almost never. If Beargrease was a drinker, he was not the rowdy kind that lost his senses and turned ugly. That might be a fair description of his brother Peter, but John reacted to alcohol in the opposite manner. Mary Lornston-Hangartner, a childhood friend of the Beargrease daughters, commented, "The more [John] drank the quieter he became. This was considered a most unusual reaction."[18]

CHAPTER FIVE

Bells in the Woods

Minnesota's annual John Beargrease Sled Dog Marathon is the most prestigious such race in the lower forty-eight states. Thanks to the marathon, the name John Beargrease is nearly synonymous with dogsled racing today. Since the early 1980s, mushers have been gathering on the North Shore in Minnesota's coldest months to run the race named after the famous mailman. Originally, the race route extended from Duluth to Grand Marais. In 1984, the distance doubled with the addition of a return trip. In 1988, the distance grew again, encompassing the frozen miles from Duluth to Grand Portage and back. The round-trip race course is now 390 miles long.

When he first began running the mail sometime around 1879, John Beargrease occasionally may have been responsible for carrying the mail over a distance like that and back, but his route did not cover that entire circuit for long. Other mail carriers were also active in the early 1880s, and they were responsible for various legs of the mail route. After the trains started running to Two Harbors, Beargrease hauled the mail from there to Grand Marais and back while Louis Plante carried it from Grand Marais to Grand Portage. Throughout most of the rest of his mail-carrying career, Beargrease remained responsible only for the route between Two Harbors and Grand Marais, a 150-mile round-trip.

Two Harbors

Before 1883, John Beargrease and the other North Shore mail

contractors did not bother stopping at Agate Bay unless it was to take shelter from a storm or spend a night. The Anishinabe called the location *Wasswewining*, allegedly meaning "Place to spear by moonlight," but there was no Indian settlement there. The only settler on Agate Bay was the reclusive Thomas Sexton, and he was usually absent. For twenty-five years after Sexton first put up his cabin, his 154-acre claim at Agate Bay remained a quiet, unsettled piece of lakeshore wilderness. For the first four years that Beargrease ran the mail route, Sexton's cabin was the lone structure at Agate Bay.

In 1882, however, all of that changed. Sexton sold all but four acres of his property to the Duluth & Iron Range Railroad, which sought to establish a harbor for the shipment of iron ore from the newly opened Vermillion iron range. Within a year, construction began. Crews of men arrived laying tracks, cutting streets and raising buildings. That same year, the railroad between Agate Bay and the Vermillion range was completed. The railroad abruptly transformed Agate Bay's remote wilderness shoreline to industrial boomtown.

The name *Two Harbors* refers to Agate Bay and the adjacent Burlington Bay, two natural harbors separated by a point of land jutting into the lake. The railroad chose Agate Bay for the iron-range railroad terminal because the bay possesses a clay bottom which facilitated the construction of the massive ore docks. If not for the rocky floor of Beaver Bay, the railroad might have chosen that place instead and fulfilled the village's wildest dreams of success. Instead, fortune passed over Beaver Bay, and Two Harbors was born.

In 1884, the first shipment of iron ore left the Two Harbors port. Towering wooden, rail-bed docks for loading iron ore stretched into the lake. A cacophony of noise, industry and progress replaced the quiet serenity of Wasswewining. Always the chug of the locomotive, the hiss of steam, the whistle of the engine, the foghorns of the great ore carriers, the shouts of the ore punchers on the docks, the rumble of iron ore pouring out of the cars, down the hoppers and into the ship's holds.

Two Harbors quickly earned a reputation as a rough town, a real Wild West city. Sexton refused to sell his remaining four acres of lakefront real estate and instead leased it out to a slew of saloons, gambling halls, dance halls and houses of ill repute, each competing in the industry of relieving railroad workers, dockworkers and lumbermen of their pay. At one point, twenty-two saloons and dance halls were crammed into those four acres. Clients dubbed Sexton's infamous property "Whiskey Row," while critics called it "Hell's Four Acres." Meanwhile, an entire town sprang up.

The weekly papers from the 1880s and 1890s give the impression of constant adventure. Hardly a week passed in which the local papers did not report on some horrible mine accident, some calamitous train wreck, some frightful dockworker injury, some dreadful maiming or some unfortunate drowning, not to mention the weekly report of a deadly fire, a Wild West-style shootout, a steamy scandal, an explosion, a shipwreck, a murder, a holdup or a robbery. The town grew too quickly for law enforcement to keep up. Stories abound of safe crackers, con-men, runaway girls in brothels, drunken lumberjacks, rowdy sailors and, of course, the infamous Whiskey Row. Apparently, it took wild men to subdue the North Shore wilderness.

For the mail service, Two Harbors became the new distribution point from which the star route serving the North Shore began. The first post office opened in 1883. In 1887, the railroad completed the line between Duluth and Two Harbors, bringing mail by rail. During the winter months, the North Shore mail found its way to Two Harbors by train, and from there the star routes carried it down the shore to Beaver Bay, Grand Marais, and Grand Portage by way of steamer, rowboat, or dog train. From then on, Two Harbors was the point from which John Beargrease began his journeys with the mail and the place to which he returned.

Beargrease Dogs

From early May to late November, John Beargrease and the other mail carriers relied on large rowboats equipped with small masts and sails. But during the winter months when the freezing waters of the lake proved to be too tempestuous to pass or when they froze over altogether, Beargrease and his colleagues fell back upon the primitive dog train to pull a toboggan loaded down with mail sacks over the snow and ice of the North Shore trail.

According to Ojibwe lore, "The dog was created in heaven itself and sent down expressly for the Indians."[1] Out of all the animals, dogs made for the highest and holiest of sacrifices. The dog was regarded as a being halfway between the animal/spiritual world and the world of human beings. The Anishinabe relied on their dogs as hunting partners, pathfinders, guardians, pack animals, family pets and companions. The dogs shared in every adventure their owners undertook.

Ancient Anishinabe legend has it that Nanaboozhoo, the first Anishinabe man, was the first to domesticate a canine. Nanaboozhoo was kinsmen to all the animals. He spoke their languages and lived at peace with them. Once, when hunting in the midst of the great forest, Nanaboozhoo was near to starvation. The wolves took pity on him, fed him and taught him their hunting secrets. When it was time for him to part ways with the wolves, the youngest wolf stayed with him. Nanaboozhoo loved the young wolf and named him Little Brother.[2]

John Beargrease had four such little brothers.

In the frozen months, the dog train was the common mode of winter transportation on the North Shore. The trails and paths that passed for roads in those days were too narrow and rugged for horse and sleigh. To get around at all in the deep snows of Minnesota winters, the pioneers and settlers learned the Ojibwe art of handling dog teams. Three or four dogs harnessed together formed a powerful pulling machine. If you are unfamiliar with dog teams, you might imagine whimpering, reluctant dogs, forced to pull against their will by the crack of the musher's whip. In reality, it is quite the opposite. Whips are almost unheard of in handling dog teams. Generally, the dogs hardly need any encouragement. They are eager to pull, and they regard the long miles of pulling as great sport. A sled dog's enthusiasm for pulling with a team is difficult to contain. It appeals to all of their natural pack inclinations. Sled dogs pull with joy.

Beargrease used four, big, mixed-breed dogs strung together to pull his mail sled while he stomped along behind on snowshoes or caught a ride by standing on the sled runners. He was proud of his dogs, occasionally posing with them for photographs, and on at least one occasion, hitching them up in midsummer for a ride down main street as part of a Two Harbors' parade. He cared for his dogs with special, doting affection.[3]

Wintry Blasts

Beargrease ran the mail in this fashion for twenty winters. He and his dogs shared innumerable adventures on the trail. They struggled together through sudden blizzards, impossibly deep snows, frigid temperatures, spring melt, heavy fogs, rain and storm.

In an address to North Shore postal employees delivered in 1933, Two Harbors postmaster, Dennis Dwan reminisced about the days when John

Beargrease was carrying the mail:

> One of the outstanding conditions of transportation which lingers in my
> memory is when our faithful servant John Beargrease transported the mail
> from Beaver Bay to Two Harbors and day or night or good weather or bad
> made no difference with John; he was sure to arrive sometime with the mail
> intact. He was known to travel day and night without food (and I was going to
> say drink but will leave that out), and when he reached his journey's end with
> his faithful dog team they would all rest up for a short time and start on the
> return trip regardless of the weather conditions. He and his dogs were known
> to be snow bound for days at a time but they would finally come through tired,
> hungry and frost bitten, but nature's wild wintry blasts had no terrors for faith-
> ful John."[4]

The occasional frostbite was inevitable. When Beargrease harnessed
the dogs for a winter mail run, the temperatures sometimes dipped more
than forty degrees below zero. The old settlers recalled winters so cold that
the woods resounded with the rifle-like reports of tree trunks freezing and
exploding. They remembered the winters of the 1880s as especially cold
and long. The winter of 1888 was particularly severe. One of the original
Two Harbors pioneers remembered ice on the bays well into May.[5]

As best we can tell from winter photographs of John Beargrease, he
dressed for the weather, in a thick fur parka, wool pants, shirt and jacket,
a warm engineer's cap and moose or deerskin mukluks on his feet.[6] On
his person, he carried a tobacco pouch, a rifle, dried meats and other
foodstuffs.[7]

Snowshoes

The deep snows of Minnesota required snowshoes. Beargrease made
his own in the Ojibwe fashion. A pair of Beargrease's snowshoes are on
display in the Lake County Historical Society museum in Two Harbors.
John and Charles Christensen presented them to the historical society
with an explanation, stating that John Beargrease himself handcrafted
them for use on the mail route:

> Beargrease made these shoes extra big. John stood about six feet, three inches
> in his moccasins, and with the extra weight of the mail bags, he needed this
> size in the soft snow. These snow shoes were entirely handcrafted. No nails,
> screws or bolts were used in their construction. They were held together by
> leather thongs, which John would renew, when they became loose from long

and heavy wear. John Beargrease shot the animals needed to keep the snow-shoes in perfect condition.[8]

The Anishinabe typically made their snowshoes of an ash-wood frame strung with close-plaited thin leather cords, the ends of which were passed around the frame and cross-beams and firmly fastened with knots. They waterproofed, treated and maintained the leather cords and strapping by applying a generous coat of bear-grease.

Whites were always amazed at the speed at which Anishinabe people could move on snowshoes. While white settlers tripped along, hopelessly clumsy in the big webbed shoes, the Anishinabe glided over the snow, ducking through the woods and over trail in a grace of motion that made the entire matter seem effortless.

So it was that once a week, John left Louise and the children to hitch up the dogs to the mail sled. Over the years, Beargrease used a variety of sleds and toboggans, depending on the amount of mail and the trail and snow conditions. At first, he used a narrow, ash-wood toboggan.[9] A finely crafted wooden dogsled alleged to once have belonged to John Beargrease is on display in the Beaver Bay Museum.

Starting Out

With his dogs straining at their gang line, eager to launch across the snow, their breath hot and steaming in the dim morning chill, Beargrease made his final preparations for the journey ahead. Their first task was to reach Two Harbors, twenty-five miles from Beaver Bay to retrieve the week's mail. When everything was in place, Beargrease climbed on board the empty mail sled and shouted a command to the dogs. They understood only Ojibwe. According to Edward Greve, "He would call to the dogs in his native tongue and they would shoot out like a shot from a gun."

If he was particularly ambitious or in a particular hurry, Beargrease could possibly arrive in Two Harbors by early afternoon where he could rest and feed the dogs, load the mail and be back to Beaver Bay some-time that evening. More likely, he would give the dogs a good rest in Two Harbors before setting out on the long journey. After all, Two Harbors' infamous Whiskey Row offered room and board and quite a bit more. Why not spend the night in town and head out for Beaver Bay in the morning?

Typically, Beargrease carried two mailbags. The lighter of the two was the letter bag. The heavier one was the media mail, a bag full of newspapers and magazines and packages. At times, Beargrease's dogs pulled as much as 700 pounds of mail. Many items were shipped overland through the mail. At one point, Louis Plante complained about having to carry an extra mail sack completely filled with horse-collar pads ordered by the Fuller Lumber Company. "He looks for a team of horses and steam engine through the mail next," the *Cook County Herald* remarked.[10]

John Beargrease was also responsible for visiting the local Two Harbors newspaper offices and collecting the papers before setting out on his journey. An 1890 issue of the *Two Harbors Iron Port* mentioned John stopping in at the newspaper office to pick up the new edition before heading off to deliver them down the shore.[11]

The Mail Trail

Finally loaded, Beargrease and the dogs set off northeast. The Lake County government maintained the trail from Two Harbors to Beaver Bay. The Cook County government was responsible for trail maintenance on its side of the county line. Board minutes from an October 1884 meeting discuss hiring men "to brush out the trail between Grand Portage and Lake county line, the same to be cleared out wide enough to allow dog trains to get through with mail… this coming winter."[12] Cutting back brush and growth, removing deadfalls and filling in washouts on the mail trail was an annual duty for the county governments. Lake County invested some effort into the trail between Two Harbors and Beaver Bay by building bridges across the major rivers between the two communities. For most of Beargrease's mail carrying career, the trail was not more than a narrow path through the woods, past Flood Bay, over the bridge across the Stewart River, inland around the Silver Cliff, over the bridges at the Gooseberry and the Split Rock Rivers, past frozen waterfalls and over uncountable numbers of streams and gullies.

Collar Bells

Modern mushers who run the John Beargrease Dogsled Marathon between Duluth and Grand Portage speak of sublime moments on the trail. The rhythmic sound of the dogs' paws on the snow, the hiss of the sled runners and the utter silence of the woods combine into something the racers describe in spiritual terms, as if the dogs have pulled them into another reality, a timeless, holy place of tree, snow, trail, shadow and light. The northern sky blazes with stars above them. The bright winter moon reflects off the snow, casting magical patterns of dark and pale light across the trail as the miles slide away beneath the runners of the sled.[13]

If the dog trail becomes a mystical journey for the modern musher, how much more so for Beargrease as week after week, mile after mile, he and his dogs ran the distance? Every jutting rock, every cutting stream, every patch of tree and forest, hill, valley, bay and cliff became familiar friends as Beargrease and his dogs traversed the shoreline trail again and again. In the winter woods of the North Shore, when there is no wind, the air becomes so quiet that a person can hear the barely audible scrush-like sound of snowflakes coming to rest one on top of another.

Beargrease's dogs filled the sublime silence about them with the constant jingle of their collar bells. All the winter mail carriers attached bells to their dog teams hoping the constant jingling would frighten off wolves and steer away moose. The early settlers told of hearing bells drifting through the woods on cold winter evenings long in advance of the mail sled's arrival.[14]

> Louie Plante arrived from Grand Portage on Monday with the first dog train of the season, and with his trained tandem dogs, jingling sleigh bells, U.S. mail, and toboggan, resembled old Santa Clause coming to town, and made a novel sight much appreciated by the youngsters. (*Cook County Herald*, December 24, 1898)

As the dog team drew close to Beaver Bay, the people of the community heard the bells and Beargrease's eager shouts to his dogs. Mary Lornston-Hangartner, one of the original Beaver Bay settler-children and a childhood friend of the Beargrease girls, reminisced about John's weekly arrival. Towards evening, she would hear Beargrease approaching town with his dog team after a long day of traversing the trail from Two Harbors.

"Bells were ringing and there was an occasional 'Hi-yi-yi' from John," she said.[15] In her memoirs she wrote, "Beargrease was really conscientious about bringing the mail through regardless of the weather. At about 7 or 8 p.m. we would hear the dogs yipping and Beargrease's weird yells as they would come charging down the big hill and draw up to the post office with a flourish."[16]

Arrival in Beaver Bay

When Beargrease first began carrying the mail as a subcontractor for the star route in 1879, the only postal stop he made between Duluth and Grand Marais was his hometown of Beaver Bay. In that respect, the mail route had not changed much since R. B. McLean carried the first mail down the shore a quarter-century earlier. Beaver Bay had not changed much either. Until the building of Two Harbors, it remained the largest settlement on the North Shore. As such, it served also as the county seat for Lake County until that honor was transferred to Two Harbors.

The Wieland brothers' handsome store on Beaver Bay Point also doubled as a home, hotel and post office. Atop the building was a distinctive cupola in which they hung a bright lantern at night to steer boats away from a dangerous piece of reef and into the safety of Beaver Bay's harbor. Sometime around 1880, Albert Wieland stepped down from his job as postmaster. A. H. Wegner, a prominent citizen and Lake County commissioner took over the Wieland store, and along with that responsibility came the post office and the position of postmaster.

As Beargrease's team drew up to the Beaver Bay post office with a flourish, Postmaster Wegner, who had been half-listening for the team's arrival, slipped on a coat and boots, lit a lantern and opened the post office. While Wegner sorted the mail and prepared the bags for the journey north, Beargrease went home. He greeted Louise and the children, unharnessed his dogs, fed and bedded them, stoked up the stove, and stripped the ice-crusted fur parka from his back. Just enough time for a hot meal and a night's sleep in his own bed, then back at the trail in the morning. The longest miles of the journey still lie ahead.

Over the Ice

The overland mail route followed a definite course maintained by Lake and Cook Counties. Nevertheless, Beargrease might alter that course at any given time depending on snow, ice and weather conditions. Streams swollen with spring flooding might necessitate a detour. When the lake's shoreline froze, Beargrease opted to travel over the surface of the ice, which offered a faster, flatter and straighter route.

Even when the ice was solid, traversing it could be a disconcerting and frightening experience. It cracked, groaned, murmured and boomed throughout the season. Though the ice could be solid many feet thick, a person could not help but feel at times that a chasm was about to open up underfoot and swallow him whole. When the weather allowed the ice to thaw, break up, and refreeze, whole fields of the shoreline become like jagged moorland scattered with enormous shards of ice standing upright—a frozen obstacle course. Cold, biting wind off the lake added to the difficulty. Even given these drawbacks, solid ice along the lake shore made the surface of the lake the preferred route by far. The entire ordeal of hills, gulleys, twisting trails and fallen trees could be avoided so long as the lake ice was solid. In most years, however, the shoreline did not freeze up until February, and in milder years, it did not freeze at all.

Often, the ice froze only in the bays or only partially. Then the lake route became hazardous in the extreme. Beargrease had to gauge the safety of the ice, learn to watch for thin patches and be alert to sudden changes. In his paper, "U.S. Mail on the North Shore," Otto Wieland of Beaver Bay described how the mail carrier was forced to change from the lake to the shore and back again many times during a trip, depending on ice conditions:

> In the winter time, the mail carrier used a dog team with a sled or a toboggan, mushing along the shore or through the woods, wherever the going was best. If the lake was frozen, and the ice safe, he would, of course, travel on the ice; but he could seldom use the ice to any extent before the beginning of February, and even after that time, he would be forced to change from the lake to the shore and back again many times during a trip. Moreover, in using the ice, it was always necessary to keep a watchful eye on the wind and weather conditions, for Lake Superior has known very few winters during which the ice floes were not frequently shifted by off shore winds, or broken up by Lake winds. Many times, the carrier found a stretch of open water where he had planned to change back to the shore.[17]

The mood of Lake Superior might suddenly change, and within a few short hours, she might break up her ice floes with wind and battering waves.

The story is told of Father Baraga, the famous Catholic missionary of Lake Superior, walking the ice of the lake from La Pointe, Wisconsin to Ontagon, Michigan when he and his companion suddenly realized that the ice on which they were walking had detached from the shore and was floating free in the lake. Rising wind and waves began to break their little iceberg apart while carrying them farther into the water. Utterly unflappable in faith, Baraga continued to walk along the now floating ice berg. His faith was rewarded. The wind shifted direction and carried him and his companion on their ice floe to their very destination.[18] But it might just as well have carried them into the middle of the lake, and the same could have happened to Beargrease as he hazarded uncertain ice.

Even when the ice was solid and stable, the ice shelves cracked at times and spread, leaving crevices of open water several feet wide. Early settlers traveling over the ice sometimes carried planks and poles to span occasional breaks. One settler told the story of how, while driving a team of horses across the ice near Two Harbors, the team slowed and stopped, despite the driver's urging. The stubborn horses refused to budge. Instead, they bent their necks and began to drink from the open water which had been completely invisible from a few yards back.[19]

In Anishinabe lore, Nanaboozhoo sternly warned his wolf companion, "My dear little brother, do not ever go near this certain lake, and never walk out on the ice." Nanaboozhoo feared the Snake King who lived at the bottom of the lake. For several days, the wolf heeded Nanaboozhoo's warning, but the matter vexed him. At length, curiosity compelled the wolf to venture onto the ice. In the middle of lake, due to the Snake King's mischief, he fell through the ice and drowned. Nanaboozhoo mourned for his little brother so loudly that one could hear it at the other end of the forest.[20]

Mail carrier Louis Plante did go through the ice, dogs and all. One January day in 1907, he decided to try crossing an iced-over bay near Hovland. The ice was not as firm as he had hoped: "Dogs, sled, mail and mailman all broke through the ice into the numbing water! Getting up and out of the water after struggling for an hour, he was able to resume his trip, with everything recovered."[21]

Beargrease inevitably experienced similar close calls as he ran the mail over Superior's treacherous ice for twenty years.

A View From the Ice

Today's North Shore tourists are generally familiar with the heart-stopping beauty of Lake Superior's rugged shore between Two Harbors and Grand Marais. When taken in from the frozen lake, the shoreline reveals a completely new grandeur. Beargrease and his dogs would cut across a frozen bay by dawn, skating along beneath the towering cliffs of the shore while the pale February sun rose over the open water on the lake. As Beargrease and his dogs sped over the smooth, snow-covered surface, the cliffs and mighty shoreline rocks frosted with snow and ice must have seemed almost magical. Numerous caves, not visible from the land, provided resting spots and shelter from the wind. In summer months, they were accessible only by boat. In the winter, the frozen lake surface gave them a fine floor. From their ceilings, massive icicles hung like stalactites, reaching from great heights to touch the surface of the ice. So long as the temperatures remained low enough, Beargrease and his dogs could shoot along the shore like water-walkers, like a spirit gliding over the surface.

For the residents along the shore, good lake ice meant easy transportation by way of sled, sleigh or even skates. Ice skating was more than recreational. The early North Shore pioneers used skates to travel quickly between settlements. The skaters kept note of their times and distances, even competing with each other and trying to set records.[22] As a young man, John Slater of Beaver Bay used to assist John Beargrease on the mail route. When he was older, he ran a portion of the route himself, occasionally using ice skates to deliver mail along the shore because the skates were faster and all the buildings to which he had to make deliveries were right along the shore.[23]

Making Time

For most of the winter, traveling on the lake ice was not an option, and John Beargrease and his dogs followed the beaten mail path. North Shore blizzards are notorious for the speed with which they drop snow, and there are tales of Beargrease and his dogs weathering blizzards "when the snow fell so fast as to obliterate the tracks of the sledge immediately after it had passed."[24] On those occasions, it was sometimes best to just keep going. In other instances, when fierce wind and snow made progress impossible, Beargrease and the dogs huddled down together and waited the storm out. A half-day later or so, they would be at it again, pushing through three feet of snow, plowing over drifts six- and seven-feet deep, making their way among the boughs of the trees as they stumbled over the wind piles.

In the complete whiteout of a blizzard or the heavy darkness of snow-choked nights or the thick blanketing fogs of the shore, Beargrease would have lost the winding trail, finding himself far off course, if not for the innate ability of the dogs to keep the path. Dogs naturally possess a keen sense of smell, a remarkable memory and an uncanny internal compass. Sled dogs learn routes quickly and never forget them. Beargrease's dogs knew the way up and down the shore, with all the variations of route. Though he traveled across hundreds of miles of uninhabited wild forest land, there was never a danger of John losing his way.

Greve speculates that Beargrease and the dogs did an average thirty to forty miles a day. The run from Beaver Bay to Grand Marais probably took two full days. According to local lore, he and the dogs once made the entire distance in twenty-eight hours.

Even making the round-trip mail run only once a week meant that Beargrease and the dogs were on the trail four to six days a week during the winter. There were bound to be a few mishaps and misadventures: "Beargrease and his huskies braved the blizzard, sleet and winrows of ice along the shoreline, and more than one rumor of his accidental death along the route was later proved false."[25]

The Mail Carrier Arrives

Whenever Beargrease pulled into a community, everyone within earshot of the sled bells gathered around the post office to greet him, check their mail, get newspapers and, most importantly, hear the latest news. The mail carrier also served as the source of information about weather, snow depth, ice thickness and trail conditions.

What's the latest in Two Harbors? How is the trapping around Beaver Bay? How many men are employed in the lumber camp now? Any word on mineral prospecting? Have they started the ice harvest up the shore? Beargrease carried more than mail.

In addition to the regular questions, good Ojibwe etiquette required a litany of inquiries into the health and welfare of family members, a protocol both Beargrease and the North Shore pioneers rehearsed week-after-week. How is your wife? Is she over that cold? I may have a remedy for that. And your father? Is he well? Is your mother still in good health? Your children? And so it went.

The mail carrier often had some adventure from the trail to relate as well: a night with wolves, a close encounter with a moose, a bear sighting, a narrow escape or harrowing traverse.

Redmyer

Even on his earliest mail runs, John Beargrease stopped to drop in on the Redmyer family. As early as 1880, the Norwegian fisherman Henry J. Redmyer had settled a claim at the mouth of the Cross River, the site of Father Baraga's miraculous traverse. The Redmyer's were principally commercial fishermen, operating a brisk fishing trade from their lonely outpost on the Superior shore. They are best remembered for building their own, sixty-five-foot fishing schooner, the Emile.

In 1888, Henry Redmyers son Hedley applied to the postal service for a post office. On March 23, 1888, he was made postmaster for the little community of Redmyer. The Redmyer post office served the tiny Cross River fishing community for three years.[26]

Lutsen

In the summer of 1885, John Beargrease was surprised to find a homestead suddenly erected at the mouth of Poplar River. Swedish settler Charles Nelson had built the shanty at his home in Duluth, carried the prefabricated sections to the Poplar River on a tug and assembled them on the shore by simply standing them up and inserting wooden pegs. Nelson was the latest contractor for the Booth Packing Company. The Booth company supplied him with a boat, nets, tackle and a loan for settling on the Poplar River. In return, his job was to supply them with plenty of fish.

In his first year at the Poplar River, Nelson built a cabin, a fish house and docks. In 1887, Charles and his wife Anna, along with their newborn son, moved into the homestead permanently. Their nearest neighbors were the Redmyers, ten miles down the shore at Cross River.

More family members from Sweden joined them in 1888. Nelson's little settlement soon boasted a community of twenty-five people—nearly half of whom were Nelsons. Nelson applied for a post office, requesting that the settlement be called Poplar River, but the Postal Service rejected the application for that name. In his second attempt, Nelson chose the name "Lutsen" in honor of the Swedish king, Gustavus Adolphus II, who was killed at the Battle of Lutzen in Saxony in 1632. On June 11, 1890, the U.S. Postal Service conceded and named Charles Nelson postmaster for the village of Lutsen.

Unfortunately for the Redmyer neighbors ten miles down the shore, the new post office at Lutsen meant the demise of their own postal station. The U.S. Postal Service could not justify two post offices within ten miles of each other serving a combined population of less than thirty settlers.

Since Lutsen boasted the larger settlement, the postmaster general closed the Redmyer office.[27]

On his way down the shore to Grand Marais, Beargrease frequently stopped for the night in Lutsen. Even in those days, Lutsen was becoming famous for hosting guests. A decade later, the Nelsons were making a business out of hospitality by hosting travelers in the second-floor of their large new home. Mrs. Anna Nelson prepared meals for the guests. "The Lutzen House is crowded with guests upon the arrival of every boat, and the weary traveler is well pleased with the spacious rooms, while the meals cannot be excelled," Nelson hyped in the *Cook County Herald*.[28]

Carl Nelson, the oldest son at Lutzen House, remembered lodging the mail carrier and his dog team. "At first we got our mail by boat in the summer and by dog team in the winter. We had many dog teams staying at our place. The dogs put up many a hard fight at times,"[29] he recalled.

Another son, George Nelson, remembered that John Beargrease earned room and board at their home for doing a few chores about the place such as carrying the heavy water buckets up from the Lake and through the snowdrifts for his mother.[30]

Grand Marais

When Beargrease and the dogs finally reached Grand Marais, they headed straight for Mayhew's trading post, a two-story building that also served as post office, schoolhouse, county courthouse and doctor's office. It stood on a neck of land on the bay of Grand Marais.

Beargrease (and all the mail carriers, for that matter) enjoyed the status of a local celebrity in Grand Marais. The residents of Grand Marais keenly felt their winter isolation, and they relied on the mail carriers as their only link to the outside world. John's arrival was a weekly celebration, anticipated and observed by the entire community.

The townsfolk gathered around the mail carrier to hear the latest news from up the shore and to grab their weekly newspapers. While the people of Grand Marais assembled to collect their mail, Beargrease loosed the dogs to feed them behind the trading post. Little Edith Mayhew, an eyewitness to the weekly ritual, recalled the entire process. Beargrease built a roaring fire that served to thaw out both himself and the dogs. Over the fire, he boiled a huge, four-legged, iron pot of cornmeal mush. Once the mush was cooked, he ladled it off into big metal pans and old pails. The boiling mush was too hot for the dogs to eat immediately, so the hungry animals solemnly stood guard over their respective servings until the food had sufficiently cooled.[31]

For most of Beargrease's mail-carrying career, Grand Marais was the turning point of his route. When pressed for time, he turned his sled back up the shore, and they headed out as soon as the dogs were fed and rested. When they had more leisure, or if daylight was short, Beargrease comfortably spent the night in Grand Marais.

He slept at the Mayhews' post. The trading post offered stick candy, canned goods, barrels of salt pork, corned beef, flour, sugar, lard, butter, bread, crackers, coffee, tea or pretty much anything you might need, though probably not exactly what you wanted. It served as the community post office until 1893 when Henry Mayhew lost his appointment as postmaster to Chris Murphy, the editor of the *Cook County Herald*.

After a night in Grand Marais, it was time to turn about, harness the dogs, head back up the trail and brave the wintry blasts once again. When setting out, he found the mail bags reloaded with southwest-bound mail for the return trip.

Moose and Wolf

How many adventures and misadventures did he share with his dogs on those long sled runs up and down the shore? Undoubtedly, he had a few moose encounters. Dog teams and moose do not mix well. The dogs have entirely too much enthusiasm about the gigantic animals. A big bull moose might resent being startled by the dog team and express his displeasure with a kick or sweep of his antlers. A Grand Marais area settler once reported being chased up a tree by a surly moose who then patiently stood watch at the base of the tree, waiting for his prey to come down or fall down. Fortunately for the frightened man in the tree, a nearby pack of wolves picked up the moose scent and came howling through the woods. The moose abandoned his post, loping off into the woods. A few moments later the wolves passed by the tree, just below the man, in hot pursuit. Shaken but unharmed, the man climbed down and hurried home.[32]

For Beargrease, an encounter with a moose on the trail would have been a welcome opportunity. He carried a rifle with him, and despite the stiff penalty for violating game laws, a moose meant food for the family.

Wolves could be a problem too. On many-a-night, the howls of their hunting packs resounded through the northwoods, unnerving the sled dogs. Most of the time, a pack of wolves showed only brief interest in a passing dog train, but when snows were deep and hunting difficult, the wolves became worrisome. When they were hungry enough, they followed the dog train, sometimes whole packs trotting along just behind the dogs. One Grand Marais man who made a dogsled trip to Duluth reported being closely followed by wolves all the way to Two Harbors.[33]

The Torrents of Spring

Despite the rigors of the frigid North Shore winters, Beargrease preferred the cold to the difficulties of the spring thaw. In April and May, the deep snows gave way to slush and mud. The solid lake ice turned rotten. Soft, wet melting snow and stretches of mud made the dog team impracticable in the spring months. So long as the lake remained impassable for mail boat, Beargrease had to carry the mail on his back.

Melting snow and spring rains swelled every stream and river crossing the path into barely passable torrents. In late April, 1908, a North Shore mail carrier attempted to cross the Popple River while it was flooded with melt-off and spring rain. The bridge had been swept away, so he tried to swim across near the mouth of the river. Instead, the stiff current dragged him out to the lake, where the waves pulled him under.[34] Such were the hazards Beargrease and his dogs endured week after week as he carried two bags full of mail—of which he could not read a single a word.

CHAPTER SIX

Mail by Sail

Today, John Beargrease is famous for having run the North Shore mail route with dog teams, but in his own day, he was also famous for carrying the mail in a rowboat. The newspapers referred to Beargrease as the "the famous half-breed pilot of Beaver Bay."[1] He earned that fame from more than a decade of braving Lake Superior's frigid waters. Like the North Shore mail carriers before him, Beargrease relied on a large rowboat, equipped with masts and sails to carry the mail up and down the shore from April to December. So long as the lake was cooperative, he preferred to the deliver the mail by rowboat before resorting to dog team. The rowboat, however, was a hazardous mode of transport, particularly in the late fall and early winter.

Lake Superior is known for her sudden mood changes. She often caresses the shore with gentle lapping waves; sometimes her surface is as calm as glass, but she might just as easily suddenly toss up thrashing breakers under the compulsion of an explosive northeaster. If the waves do not overturn the boatman, dumping him into the icy cold depths until his limbs lock up from hypothermia and the lake swallows him whole, the wind and wave might still smash him up against the rocks, breaking him on the rugged shore, shattering his boat and splintering his bones open on the stones. Every year, the lake claimed several lives.

Even without capsizing or striking the rocks, the rain, wind, driving snow and spraying waves of the lake can still claim lives. Corpses have been found still afloat in their crafts, frozen stiff. The old fishermen tell plenty of stories of having one's hands frozen to the oars or having one's feet frozen into the ice on the boat's bottom. They tell stories of having to use axes to chop men free.

Each shuttle down the shore and back made for an adventure fraught with peril and challenge. An unfavorable wind meant endless straining at the oars. High waves required constant vigilance, lest the lake sweep the little craft against the unforgiving rocks and cliffs of the shoreline.

Small craft like the mail boats rarely ventured too far out into the water. As Beargrease carried the mail up the shore towards Two Harbors and down the shore towards Grand Marais, he stayed close to the shoreline, ready to head in for land if the weather should turn too rough. In order to make the best possible time, Beargrease stayed at the oars day and night, lest the weather turn for the worse and force him ashore, stranding both him and the mail. When forced ashore, he might be pinned down by a storm for a day or so before the lake calmed enough to let him pass. There on some isolated strip of beach or pulled up among the stones and boulders of the shore, he would take shelter from the wind, rain, sleet and snow beneath the hull of his overturned boat. Otto Weiland describes camping on the beech while on the mail route waiting for the lake to calm:

> Since bad weather was apt to tie the carrier up en route at almost any time, he found it advisable to cover as much ground, in this case water, as he possibly could while the weather was favorable, and therefore he would often stick to his oars for much of the night.
>
> Along the greater portion of the shore, settlements were few and far between, and when he felt the need of rest, he would select a convenient gravel beach for his lodging. If the weather was good, he would sleep on the open beach, under the stars; if it rained, or the weather was otherwise inclement, he would sleep under his overturned rowboat, if necessary keeping a small fire alive just within reach of his arm. An abundant supply of driftwood was always to be found on these beaches, and, if he expected to be tied up for several days… he would collect a quantity of fire wood under his boat. [2]

Burlington Bay

John Beargrease's mail voyages began from Burlington Bay, the northern-most of the two natural harbors for which Two Harbors was named. In those days a natural stone arch reached into the lake from the eastern end of Burlington Bay, east of Fisherman's Point. The stone arch was a popular attraction for sightseers and day-boaters around Two Harbors. The beginning of Beargrease's weekly voyage took him under the arch or just around it, and it served as a great gate into *Kitchi Gami's* domain. The arch, as well as the entire point of land on which it was once located, has long since crumbled and disappeared.[3]

After passing through the arch in his mail-laden boat, his course took him northeast along the shore. The way down the shore toward Grand Marais from Two Harbors is rich in natural wonder and sweeping beauty. Ancient volcanic action laid up great piles of cliff and stone, scraped bare by glaciers and worn by crashing waves. In Beargrease's day, the rises beyond that rocky shore were still cloaked in the vast and ancient forest of the northwoods. As Beargrease worked his way northeast down the shore, he passed by several spots which are popular tourist destinations today, but most modern tourists completely miss the other side of the North Shore's scenery—the view from the water. From the water, a whole new face of the shore is suddenly visible: little bays and landings, towering cliffs, offshore islands, river mouths, stacks of boulders—all concealed from the view of the modern motorist. Such was Beargrease's weekly commute.

Castle Danger, Gooseberry and Splitrock

Eleven miles out of Two Harbors, Beargrease put in briefly for a stop at Castle Danger, a small Norwegian fishing settlement that became a logging center during the lumber harvest of the late 1890s. According to local lore, it is named Castle Danger because the cliffs along the shore resemble a castle's walls, or, alternatively, because a boat named *The Castle* once ran aground there. Lumberjacks collected and tied logs at Castle Danger to form huge rafts for towing to sawmills. As Beargrease rowed his way around these mile-wide rafts of tree trunks bobbing on the water, he must have been shocked at the ruthless efficiency of the lumber industry and its gluttonous toll on the land.

Two miles further, Beargrease rowed past the gentle sloping lava formations at the mouth of the Gooseberry River. According to one local legend, the river is named after the French explorer Sieur des Groseillers, which apparently translates to "Gooseberry." Another explanation identifies Gooseberry as a translation of the Ojibwe name *Shab-on-im-i-kan-i-sibi*, which is said to mean "The Place of Gooseberries River."[4] Today, a wayside rest stop and state park featuring the river's spectacular waterfalls attracts thousands of annual visitors.

Four miles beyond Gooseberry, Beargrease sailed past the mouth of the Split Rock River. The welcoming gravel beach may have provided a good place for him to put in if necessary. The origin of the name is uncertain, but according to some theories, it is named for a curious rock formation near the river's source.[5] According to Fritzen's *North Shore Historical Map*, the Anishinabe name for the river is *Gin-on-wab-i-ko-zibi*, meaning "War-Eagle-Iron-River."[6] Around the turn of the century, the Split Rock River became a major lumber center with railroads and steamers hauling away the North Shore's forests at an alarming speed.

Three miles past the mouth of the Split Rock River, his mail boat skirted beneath the massive bluff atop which the famous Split Rock lighthouse now sits, but Beargrease never saw the lighthouse completed. Construction on the lighthouse did not begin until 1909, only a year before his death and a decade after he had retired from the mail route. As he ran errands between Two Harbors and Beaver Bay, he would have seen the amazing construction operation taking place on the bluffs above, but he did not live to see the beacon lit or to hear its mournful foghorn.

From Split Rock Bluff, Beargrease had only four more miles to complete the first leg of his journey. He and the mail carriers of his day were not the only brave souls that frequented the twenty-five miles between Two Harbors and Beaver Bay. The residents of Beaver Bay regularly took rowboats to and from Two Harbors to procure supplies and conduct business. The rowboat was their most common mode of transportation, far faster than traveling overland on the difficult roads.

Beaver Bay and Palisade

As Beargrease rounded the Beaver Bay point by night and rowed into the welcoming harbor of his hometown, his eyes searched for the light of the great lantern hanging in the cupola of the general store and post office. It was the closest thing to a lighthouse that Beaver Bay ever had.

Arrival at Beaver Bay meant that the first twenty-five miles of his journey were completed, but the greater part of the distance still remained ahead of him. The mail contract allotted him forty-eight hours to cover the sixty additional miles to Grand Marais. Beargrease rarely needed forty-eight hours though. If he stayed at the oars through the night, and so long as the weather cooperated, he could cover the distance in just over half that time.

About five miles down the shore from Beaver Bay, Beargrease passed beneath the towering cliff walls of Palisade Head, a sheer height of 320 feet. As a boy, he would have clambered over those spectacular heights harvesting the wild blueberries which grow in abundance on top of the lichen-covered stone. According to local Anishinabe lore, a man who could shoot an arrow from the surface of the water and land it atop the cliff was guaranteed a long life. In his reminiscences, H. P. Wieland related the tradition:

> Before the time of the white settlement at Beaver Bay, the Indians used to gather here in the summer, and on a certain day when the lake was calm would shoot their arrows from their canoes straight up and he who would land an arrow on top of the cliff would live to a very old age. I knew only one Indian who accomplished this. His name was Shawabiness (Yellowbird), but he did not become very old. He died at Beaver Bay about 1880 at the age of 65 years.[7]

At the base of those cliffs, a small stream called the Palisade Creek empties into the lake. Beargrease was as familiar with the Palisade Creek as he was with the Beaver River along which he had grown up. He trapped and hunted along the Palisade Creek's twisting path all the way inland to its source at Tettagouche Lake. In later years, he owned a parcel of land a half-mile from its course.[8]

Baptism River and Crystal Bay

Only three miles down the shore from the Palisade Creek mouth, the Baptism River flows into the lake at one of the most scenically beautiful spots on Lake Superior. The Baptism River mouth and the jutting peninsula of Shovel Point all fall within Tetagouche State Park and are frequented by tourists today, but in Beargrease's day, only a handful of settlers lived at the mouth of the river.

Rounding Shovel Point, Beargrease passed by Crystal Bay where only a few years after his retirement he would see the nascent 3M Company's crushing plant and dock in operation. In the days of his mail route, however, Crystal Bay would have looked just as it does today, a rocky stretch of uninhabited beach flanked by splendid rock formations.

Little Marais and Manitou

Six miles beyond Crystal Bay, Beargrease put in at Little Marais where a lumber camp operated. In his later years, this lumber camp was abandoned and the old camp buildings were inhabited by some Norwegian settlers. Beargrease used to call on the settlers there.

Another two miles down the shore, he rowed past the mouth of the Manitou (Spirit) River. The Manitou features the only straight-drop waterfall directly into Lake Superior. A rock archway and mammoth cave complete the spiritual grandeur of the place. Unfortunately for land-based tourists, the mouth of the Manitou is private property.

Three miles beyond the Manitou River, he passed the mouth of the Caribou River and into Cook County. He sailed along a beautiful stretch of rocky shoreline, past several small offshore islands such as Sugar Loaf at Sugar Loaf Cove and Gull and Bear islands at Two Island River.

Cross and Temperance Rivers

Nine miles into Cook County, Beargrease rowed his way into harbor at the mouth of the Cross River where the Redmyer family settled and, after 1896, the Schroeder Lumber Company operated. According to Fritzen, the Ojibwe name for the river is *Tchibaiatigo* which he understands to mean "Wood of the Soul or Spirit River."[9] Fritzen says that Anishinabe regularly navigated the Tchibaiatigo by way of canoe to traverse between Lake Vermillion and the North Shore. If so, Beargrease certainly made that journey himself a few times.

The name Cross River derives from the celebrated miracle of Father Baraga's traverse over the lake. In 1846 Father Baraga, the famous Catholic missionary of Lake Superior, set out from La Pointe on an emergency mission to Grand Portage. He was in a small fishing boat, similar to the type of craft the North Shore mail carriers used. Due to the urgency of his task, he decided to attempt to cross the lake directly rather than hug the shore all the way around. Though his Ojibwe companion tried to deter him from such a foolish course, he insisted. The lake was calm when they set out, but they were not yet halfway when a strong wind arose. As Father Baraga's companion feared, the lake turned into a churning fury of seething water, and their little craft was driven by the wind. Utterly unflappable, Baraga immersed himself in his prayer book, paying little heed to the wind and waves around him.

Miraculously, the boat did not capsize, but as they approached the opposite shore, a new danger appeared. The tossing waves were throwing up great breakers against a craggy shoreline, and there was no hope of safely mooring the craft. They were certainly about to be smashed against the rocks. Still Baraga remained unconcerned and instructed his companion to steer straight ahead into the rocky shore. Amazingly, the craft was tossed through the breakers and into the mouth of the *Tchibaiatigo* river. The missionary then closed his prayer book, stepped ashore and built a small wooden cross to commemorate the miraculous traverse. The river was henceforth called the Cross River.

The story was well-known and celebrated even in Beargrease's day. Today, tourists can walk down to the mouth of the river and see a permanent monument placed in memoriam of Father Baraga's cross and his amazing traverse.[10]

A mile beyond the Cross River, Beargrease sailed past the mouth of the Temperance. The name of the river is a subtle joke. Most of the rivers and streams that empty into the lake are blocked at the mouth by a stone and gravel sandbar. Since this particular river had no "bar" at its mouth, it was given the name Temperance. A state park makes it possible today for North Shore visitors to enjoy the Temperance, with its frightening waterfalls and magnificent beach.

Carlton Peak to Grand Marais

Two more miles down the shore, Beargrease passed Carlton Peak, a tall hilltop and obvious landmark from the water. Today, the location is home to the community of Tofte.

Beargrease had seven miles from Carlton Peak to the mouth of the Poplar River. According to Fritzen, the Anishinabe name for the Poplar river is *Ga-Man-A-Za-Di-Ka*,[11] perhaps an Ojibwe equivalent of Poplar River, but Fritzen offers no direct translation. Beargrease rowed to shore where he would find the Nelson family and the Lutsen community waiting for the mail.

Another twelve miles down the shore, past the generous flow of the Cascade River which is named for its series of cascading waterfalls, John Beargrease finally arrived at Grand Marais, his last destination before turning around and heading home. Beginning in 1885, Grand Marais began operating a lighthouse to guide ships into its harbor. When rowing in heavy fog, Beargrease heard the steady toll of the lighthouse fogbell as he drew close to the harbor. Joseph Mayhew, the younger brother of Postmaster Henry Mayhew, served as the lighthouse keeper.

If Beargrease had made good time, he could rest at least a full night before heading back, but if he was behind schedule, he might make due with only a few hours of sleep before climbing back in the boat and facing the wind and waves again.

Troubled Waters

Rough weather on the lake was always an imminent danger, and Beargrease was not the only mail carrier subject to the lake's risks. The *Cook County Herald* tells a dramatic mail boat story that almost spelled the end of Louis Plante's mail carrying career:

> Mail Carrier Louis Plante had a very narrow escape from a watery grave last Friday. He was en route to Grand Portage from Hovland when off Howard's Point a heavy sea combined with a gale of wind capsized his boat. He managed to climb on top of it and hold on until John Drouillard, who witnessed the occurrence, could reach him… Louis has a dangerous route at best and during the stormy weather which has prevailed this year the place has been especially hard and dangerous. (*Cook County Herald*, August 5, 1899)

Despite the hazards of the lake, the mail boat was always the preferred method of mail carrying. So long as the voyage seemed plausible, Beargrease opted for the mail boat over the dog team or other mode of travel.

Like the mail carriers, North Shore fishermen of the time were known for taking risks on Lake Superior, even in the dangerous waters of the winter months. It often happened that a man in a small craft like a mail boat found himself stranded on the water. As he tried to bring his boat into harbor, the wind and drag of the undertow forced him back, relentlessly seeking to carry him out into the deep water. A man might spend hour upon grueling hour, soaked through and through, chilled to the bone, waging a losing fight for his life against the wind and waves.

If by luck someone on shore sighted him, they would attempt a rescue with great lengths of rope and another boat. The rescuers tied one end of the rope securely on land and carried the other end with them out to the floundering craft. If the rope afforded them enough length to reach the party, they used it to pull themselves and the stranded boat back to the safety of the shore. After twenty years of mail by sail, John Beargrease must have experienced similar rescues, on some occasions playing the role of rescuer and at other times that of the rescued.

Passengers

Beargrease routinely had company in his mail boat. In most of the mail boat anecdotes, two carriers are in the boat. Having an extra hand along to take a turn at the oars increased speed. John's younger brothers often helped him haul the mail both in summer and winter and sometimes made the entire mail run on his behalf. His younger brother Gageget Jumuson once made the trip from Beaver Bay to Grand Marais in a record twenty hours.[12]

On other occasions, Beargrease picked up a passenger or two hitching a ride up or down the shore. Charles Nelson, the proprietor and postmaster at Lutsen, was known to catch a ride to Grand Marais for business trips and social calls.[13] On one such trip, due to an embarrassing mishap for rookie mail carrier Koss, both the mail carrier and Mr. Nelson found themselves forced to walk back from Grand Marais:

> Postmaster Nelson of Lutsen came down with mail carrier Koss in a rowboat Wednesday for a short visit with his friends here. During the storm on the lake Thursday forenoon their boat was washed off the beach where they had left it and was dashed to pieces on the rocks, necessitating their return on the trail Thursday evening. (*Cook County Herald*, March 31, 1894)

The story illustrates how the mail boat still faced some jeopardy from the lake even while safely pulled ashore.

Competition

In 1890, the Booth Packing Company won the contract for carrying the mail through the navigational season. Apparently, Henry and Thomas Mayhew of Grand Marais petitioned the Postmaster General to upgrade the celerity, certainty and security of the mail route by establishing regular steamer service. When the 1890 navigation season opened, the Booth Company's steamer *Dixon* began carrying the summertime mail, making two full roundtrips between Duluth and Port Arthur every week.

The regular steamer deliveries were a vast improvement. The steamer service gave the remote pioneers of Grand Marais a sense of connection with the outside world. More than bringing regular mail, the weekly arrival of the steamer made a quick and comfortable trip to Duluth and back a possibility. Throughout the navigational season, the Grand Marais newspaper religiously reported on the comings and goings of the local residents as they constantly boarded and disembarked from the *Dixon*.

As the *Dixon* arrived at Grand Marais each week, she announced her arrival with a blast of the steam whistle. The whole town, it seemed, would drop whatever they were doing and hurry to the dock, crowding around the arriving steamer, eager for news, mail and packages, just as they had come to welcome the winter mail carrier when they heard the ringing of his sled bells.

Not every stop along the route, however, had a harbor and dock to accommodate steamer service. More remote locations such as Lutsen and Tofte made delivery from the steamer far more difficult. Community members had to row out into the lake to meet the steamer and transfer mail, supplies and passengers. Livestock deliveries were forced to swim ashore.

So long as the navigational season remained open, the pioneers of Lake and Cook Counties felt comparatively cosmopolitan. Thanks to the Dixon, they were well connected with the rest of the world and could come and go as they pleased. Each fall, as the *Dixon* pulled away from the Grand Marais docks for the last time, the lonely sense of isolation immediately returned. The local paper always took note of the ship's last departure:

> From now 'till May 15th we will receive mail from the outside world only once a week, the Dixon's season for carrying the mail having expired the 31st. As in former years the mail will be carried in rowboat from Two Harbors so long as the lake remains open, after which time it will be carried over the trail by dog train. (*Cook County Herald*, November 2, 1895)

> With the return of the Dixon to Duluth last Tuesday, navigation along the North Shore closed for the season. A little walk of 86 miles is all that now separates us from the outside world. (*Cook County Herald*, December 5, 1896)

> Returning to Duluth the Dixon left here Wednesday evening on her last trip of the season. Being shut off from the outside world we can now settle ourselves in for five months of peace and quietude. (*Cook County Herald*, December 4, 1897)

When the *Dixon's* first summer of carrying the mail ended, the star route service returned to Beargrease for the winter months. The *Two Harbor's Iron Port* took note, "Bear Grease, the famous half-breed pilot of Beaver Bay, left here last Saturday. He will proceed on to Grand Marais a distance of 75 miles. He called on the Iron Port for the papers that go to the subscribers at those towns."[14]

A Desperate Bid

As much as the *Dixon*'s regular mail delivery was a boon to the Grand Marais settlers, it was a great setback for the Beargrease family. The regular earnings from year-round employment to which they were accustomed were suddenly compromised—a loss of five months' income. When the steamer *Dixon* first took over the summer mail route in the year 1890, Beargrease was a father of three young daughters: Charlotte, Mary and Constance. He tried to compensate for the loss of summer income with other work. In the summer of 1890, he worked as a commercial fisherman. The next summer, John hired himself out as a claim locator and guide:

> Bear Grease, of Beaver Bay, who has been locating several of our citizens on pine land claims back of that place, returned home on the Dixon Sunday... Mr. Geo. Munford, Fred. Woodward, and John Dahn have been located on fine claims back of Beaver Bay, by Bear Grease, the famous half-breed pilot of the North Shore. (*Two Harbors Iron Port*, June 4, 1891)

In addition to fishing and claim locating, Beargrease continued hunting, trapping and trading, patching together an income for his family as best he could, but he did not lose sight of the lucrative summer mail route. In the summer of 1891, he collaborated with George Hogobone of Two Harbors to underbid the *Dixon*'s star route.[15] The postal service apparently seized on the opportunity to save money and accepted the lower bid.

Offering the postmaster general a significantly lower contract price than the *Dixon* was easy for two men and a rowboat, but matching the *Dixon*'s upgraded delivery schedule proved far more difficult. The new summer mail route required a trip all the way from Two Harbors to Grand Portage and back, twice a week—an ambitious plan for just two men.

The residents of the North Shore, who had only just become accustomed to the new, twice-a-week steamer service, were dismayed at the prospect of losing it. According to the *Grand Marais Pioneer*, the Mayhew brothers were not at all amused with Beargrease's successful underbid:

> Bear Grease, the renowned half-breed pilot of the north shore is a candidate for 'rowboat mail carrier' after the Dixon's contract expires. He carried the mail for a number of years, and seldom missed a trip. Bear Grease is a reliable fellow, but we hope some arrangements may be made for continued steamboat service, as the row and sailboat plan is too slow for Cook County and the 19th century. T. W. and H. Mayhew, who worked so hard for mail steamboat service,

and finally accomplished the same, do not believe in looking backward in that direction and do not intend to do so if it can possibly be avoided. In the mail line, our people have some rights that should be respected and upheld... The Dixon now brings the mail every Sunday and Thursday from Duluth. (*Grand Marais Pioneer,* June 6, 1891)

In spite of the public outcry over their undercut, Beargrease and Mr. Hogobone made an earnest attempt to fulfill their obligation. They may have alternated the trips, requiring each man to make the great distance only once a week, or perhaps they divided the route. Even so, the arduous miles up and down the shore on a delivery schedule originally plotted for a steamer proved to be too much of an ordeal for only two men and a row-boat. They found it impossible to meet the same schedule as the steamer. Nor did the lake cooperate. The July 18 edition of the Grand Marais paper reported "heavy seas" forcing rowboats to remain ashore. Less than two months after taking over the route, the *Pioneer* reported that Beargrease was going to be giving up the contract:

> We learn that Bear Grease has decided to give up the mail contract, and he has just ascertained by bitter experience, what everybody knew some time ago— viz: That he could never carry the mail at sum given him by the star route men. May he profit by the severe lesson, and in the mean time our people pray most devoutly for better mail service. (*Grand Marais Pioneer,* July 30, 1891)

One week later, the rumor was confirmed. The August 6 edition of the newspaper reported the official announcement. Beargrease had "thrown up his contract," and the *Dixon* was already delivering the mail again:

> Last Sunday evening our people were very agreeably surprised to receive their mail on the steamer Dixon again, Bear Grease having thrown up his contract. It is to be hoped that some arrangements will be made whereby mail service may be continued by that boat. (*Grand Marais Pioneer,* July 30, 1891)

Beargrease had gambled and lost, and he lost badly. Not only did he lose the summertime mail route to the Booth Packing Company, but he also lost the entire star route contract, including the wintertime mail route.

Over the next two years, John Beargrease was out of the mail business entirely unless he was somehow able to retain the short winter route between Two Harbors and Beaver Bay.[16] Even if that were the case, the loss of income must have been devastating to the family.

CHAPTER SEVEN

Off the Trail

Beyond his prowess as a mail carrier, John Beargrease was well known for his ability as a trapper and fur-trader. Only a month or so after giving up the mail contract, he was back in Grand Marais. The *Grand Marais Pioneer* reported, "John Beargrease, the famous North Shore pilot and mail carrier, arrived from Duluth this week, and is trading with the Indians."[1] Arriving from Duluth meant that he arrived aboard the steamer *Dixon*, the very boat to which he had lost the mail route. Trading with the Indians meant he was trading for furs collected by local Ojibwe. When he had amassed a sufficient supply of peltry, Beargrease returned to Duluth and sold it at market rates.

By the days of John Beargrease, the once lucrative fur trade had slowed down to a trickle. Years of over-trapping had thinned the population of furbearers to a critical low. Although in years past the North Shore communities of Grand Marais and Grand Portage had been thriving fur posts, and Grand Portage the center of the Northwest Company's fur trading operation, by Beargrease's day the glory of the fur trade was a distant memory. North Shore setters often ran trap-lines and did some trading to supplement their incomes, but very few people still made a sufficient living from trapping or trading.

Even still, Beargrease was in a unique position to benefit from the remnants of the fur trade. His years of running the mail made him familiar with everyone, both Indian and settler, up and down the shore. He knew who was trapping and where. He knew both Ojibwe and white culture and could move effortlessly between them. He was the perfect middleman between Anishinabe fur trappers and white traders.

Trapping on the North Shore

In addition to collecting and trading furs, Beargrease was well acquainted with handling trap-lines and preparing pelts himself. He had learned these traditional skills from his father. Trappers worked trap-lines during the late fall and winter months when the animals' furs had thickened to withstand the cold. A typical trap-line might be several miles long, and the trapper's job required him to tromp back and forth on snowshoes, up and down the line, checking for catches. Once an unhappy creature stepped into a trap, it had to be dispatched and skinned before it froze stiff. The icy cold winters of the North Shore required that a trapper keep vigilant watch over his traps. Beargrease kept outlying cabins so he could be attentive to his trap-lines.[2] His dogs, once necessary for the winter mail route, proved useful for hauling supplies and pelts up and down the trap-line and to his cabin and back.

Among the hapless furbearers that would have stepped into his traps were muskrat, fisher, marten, mink, weasel, skunk, otter, red-fox, bear and beaver. The *Lax Lake County Advocate* recorded some of his catches, "John Beargrease, the old Indian hunter and trapper, caught several fine otter and mink eight miles north of here this week."[3] Beaver, of course, was one of most valuable pelts, and its tail made a delicious soup for the family.

Anishinabe trappers like Beargrease did not always rely on iron-jawed traps for catching beaver. Kohl describes a more traditional method for catching beavers which Beargrease and his dogs may have employed. The trapper begins by opening a breach in a beaver dam on a frozen pond and draining the lake. He crisscrosses the breach with poles, creating a lattice through which the water may pass, but beavers may not. As the pond drains, the ice sheet begins to collapse, and the frightened beavers make for the escape hole in the dam where they fall prey to the waiting hunter. Dogs are positioned around the lake to watch for clever beavers that may employ an alternate escape route. Whether Beargrease employed the method or not, he would have known of it from a famous tale about Nanaboozhoo, the first Anishinabe.

It seems that in the days of Nanaboozhoo, Lake Superior was nothing but a giant beaver pond presided over by the Beaver King. One winter, Nanaboozhoo decided to catch the Beaver King and his associates. He waited until the lake froze over and then opened a breach in the eastern bank that separated Lake Superior from Lake Huron, thereby forming the Sault de St. Marie.

When Beargrease caught a beaver, he skinned it and stretched the pelt over a willow hoop, lashing it tightly with rawhide laces. Once stretched and lashed, the hide was ready for curing. After dispatching a smaller animal like a fisher or martin, he would have first impaled the sorry creature on an upright stick. Then, carefully cutting the skin free from the bottom, cautious not to remove the tail, gingerly cutting the feet free, he peeled the skin like a man peels a sock from his foot. Handling his knife like a skilled surgeon, he would have been careful to cut around the eyes and ears, considering that a premium pelt has both intact. Once he had the pelt off, inside-out, it was perfectly positioned for cleaning. Nothing was better for scraping excess fat and tissue from a pelt than the dry shoulder bone of a deer. All the meat and fat needed to be scraped off, and with hungry dogs at hand, none of it went to waste.

Beargrease cut and shaped various stretchers for the different animals' skins. Cedar slats made fine stretching boards for weasels, mink, fox, skunk and muskrat. He could use a thin, smooth wedge to stretch the fur still more and to release the skin from the board when it was dry enough to remove. Once the skins were stretched, he brought them back to his trapper's cabin and smoked them according to the traditional method of curing hides.

Road to Greenwood Lake

A trapper would trap an area until the furbearers became scarce, perhaps working a single trap-line for several weeks.[4] Apparently, Beargrease had several such trap-lines.

According to one report, John Beargrease had trap-lines as far out as Greenwood Lake toward Ely, Minnesota.[5] A partially built road once ran in that direction between Beaver Bay and Greenwood Lake.[6] The Minnesota State Legislature had passed an act authorizing the construction of a state road from Beaver Bay to Lake Vermillion in 1866.[7] Rumors of gold and mineral riches in northern Minnesota had prompted the legislature to appoint the Wieland brothers as road commissioners with the responsibility of building a road that would be passable by stagecoach. Working with a group of investors, the Wielands set to work cutting a road along the old

Greenwood Trail, which spanned the seventy-some miles between Beaver Bay and Lake Vermillion. They made it as far as Greenwood Lake where they constructed a warehouse, but then their funding suddenly collapsed. The project was abandoned. The teenaged H. P. Wieland spent the winter of 1866-1867 alone in that warehouse as he traded the remaining supplies from the failed venture with local Indians.

By the time Beargrease was traveling back and forth between Greenwood Lake and Beaver Bay some twenty to thirty years later, the Wieland road must have been overgrown and all but impassable to anyone but an experienced woodsman. For a tracker and pathfinder like Eshquabi, however, the old Wieland path would have made a fine trail. Beargrease was familiar with every old path and overgrown trail in Lake County, and the old Wieland road provided a natural route to the interior where Beargrease kept his trap-lines. A medical record from 1901 lists Beargrease's place of residence as Ely,[8] suggesting that he occasionally spent winters there tending his trap-lines.

According to an unsubstantiated rumor, John Beargrease had some help maintaining the Greenwood Lake trap-lines. Two Harbor's centennial book makes reference to an unnamed woman on Greenwood Lake who watched his traps for him in his absence and even suggests that she was a lover.[9] Beargrease possibly did have a paramour (or even a second wife) awaiting him at Greenwood Lake.

After a successful season of trapping, Beargrease piled his sled high with bales of peltry, hooked up his dogs and set out for Duluth where he could sell them. Some furs, such as a valuable fisher, could fetch as much as ten dollars.[10]

Wolf pelts were not worth much in trade, but in later years they did bring a fair price from the government. The settlers regarded wolves as a dangerous nuisance. Overhunting had thinned moose and deer populations, and caribou had already vanished from the North Shore. The settlers blamed the wolves, and the wolves may have contributed to the problem. They were numerous. Beginning in 1899, the government offered a generous bounty per kill to help curb the wolf populations,[11] thereby giving the sharp-shooting Beargrease an opportunity to profit.

"Old Indian Hunter"

Beargrease also sustained his family as a hunter. He had a reputation as a skilled hunter with uncanny abilities. As an Ojibwe, the son of an Ojibwe chief, Eshquabi's talents for tracking, stalking and bagging game were only natural. One settler told the story of how Beargrease once borrowed two small bullets, went out hunting and returned shortly with a deer.[12] Another story that has been attributed to him comes from the journal of an early Minnesota pioneer by the name of Harold Strang:

> Over the years, John [Beargrease] taught me all about Indian lore, and how to make bows and arrows, canoes, and especially how to hunt and fish. I learned from him how to read the signs of mink, muskrat, beaver, fox, otter and wolf. John was also the best hunter I ever knew. Once when we went into the woods together, three deer started across a slashing with leaps and bounds, then disappeared. John stood perfectly still and after a few moments raised his rifle toward some brush. I looked as hard as I could and I never saw them, but then John fired and got two of the three deer with just two bullets. It was always like that. He never missed. And when I asked him how he did it, he just shrugged and said he could smell them.[13]

Undoubtedly, Beargrease would have preferred to shoot a moose and bring that home for his family and neighbors, but by the year 1891 moose had suffered so much overhunting along the North Shore that they had become scarce. Government game laws forbade moose hunting, and anyone convicted of killing a moose could be fined between ten and a hundred dollars or face ten to sixty days in jail. Not that laws like this actually stopped settlers from taking down moose. They just had to be more careful about it. One settler recalled that when the game wardens were around, Beargrease was afraid to come and hunt near her family's property.[14]

Some of the early settlers employed a method of hunting which made no distinction between deer, moose or man. They set gun traps in the woods along deer trails, hoping that a passing deer would pull a tripwire and trigger a gun that had been left positioned, locked and loaded. While hunting and trapping, Beargrease would have had to remain ever-vigilant lest he snag a tripwire or step into a bear trap.

Bear Trapping

Bear trapping was common in those days. Carl Nelson, the oldest son of Charles Nelson at the Lutzen House reminisced about the bear trapping techniques he and his father employed. Since the old-time bear traps were too heavy to pack around in the woods, they devised a lighter weight version which they would secure by chaining to a ten-foot log. When a bear stepped in the trap, he would drag the log behind him. The bear could drag the log some distance, but he could not get far before the trapper caught up to him and dispatched him. Charles Nelson trapped as many as twenty-five bears a year this way, butchering them, packing their meat on ice and shipping them to market on the *Dixon*.[15]

Carl recalled a close call he had while hunting bear as a young boy. While tracking a bear who had stepped into a trap, young Carl and his father split up. His father hoped to circle around a thicket and cut the bear off. Carl was not armed, so when he found himself suddenly face-to-face with the bear, he could do nothing but shout for his father. The bear lunged at him, and the chain broke free from the drag log. Fortunately for Carl, the bear did not notice his new freedom until it was too late. Charles arrived with the rifle, and the Nelsons had another bear to drag home.[16]

In Anishinabe culture, bears were fair game. As mentioned previously, John's father, Chief Beargrease, attempted to take down a bear once by hand. No doubt John brought home the occasional bear strapped on the dogsled, a source of meat, warm fur and the ever valuable bear-grease.

Fishing

The Scandinavian settlers along the North Shore depended heavily on fishing. They knew fishing and brought their techniques with them from the old country. Fish-buying industries, such as the Booth Packing Company in Duluth, promoted commercial fishing by extending credit and lending equipment to fishermen along the shore and by providing a guaranteed market for the catch. They sent their steamships up and down the shore once or twice a week to collect the fish harvest. The same steamer *Dixon* that replaced John Beargrease on the summer mail route was responsible for picking up crates of packed fish from the fishermen along the shore and on Isle Royale.

By the 1880s, the Booth Packing Company had as many as 150 fishermen working the lake. Between 1880 and 1885, North Shore fishermen processed, salted and shipped over a half-million pounds of whitefish.[17] By the turn of the century, the number of fishermen had increased to more than 400 on the North Shore alone.[18] Records from the year 1905 indicate 146 million pounds of trout were fished out of the lake in a single year. The supply of fish seemed inexhaustible. It was not.

Long before the first settlers and Scandinavian fishermen began working the shore, the Anishinabe were harvesting Lake Superior's abundant supply of fish, relying on fish as their food-staple. In those days before commercial fishing and the introduction of foreign species, the waters teemed with three types of trout, as well as sturgeon, pickerel, pike, black bass, herring and whitefish. Anishinabe women wove long nets of nettle-stalk fiber. Using wood floats and stone sinkers, men in canoes set the nets in huge semicircles around spawning grounds. They either smoked the massive catches or hung them by their tails to dry. The dried fish provided food for the winter.[19]

Nels Eklund told of learning to make fish traps from John's cousins, the Beargrease family of Fond du Lac. He recalled weaving nets of nettle-stalk twine and stringing them across small streams with cedar floats and stone sinkers.

On other occasions the Anishinabe speared fish at night from canoes by the light of torches. Lake Superior Anishinabe were also adept at spearing fish in the winter through holes they bored in the lake ice. Many a surprised sturgeon beneath Lake Superior's ice found itself suddenly jabbed through and pulled to the surface. The Beargrease family was familiar with the traditional fishing methods and probably utilized them frequently.

A connection between Lake Superior fishing and the origin of beargrease exists in Anishinabe legend. Once it happened that Nanaboozhoo set out on Lake Superior to catch the Fish King, the great lord of the lake. He cast a hook and line but pulled up only a shiny trout. "You are not the fish I want," he said and cast it back. He cast again and pulled up a speckled *siskawet*. "You are not the fish I want," he said and cast it back. "I am fishing for the Fish King himself." Hearing his words from the depths of the lake, the gigantic Fish King decided to teach Nanaboozhoo a lesson. He swam up below his canoe and swallowed it whole with Nanaboozhoo inside, but the clever fisherman was not so easily defeated. He commenced to perform a hero's song and dance in the belly of the fish until the Fish King attempted to expel him. As the fish tried to bring him up, Nanaboozhoo lodged his canoe crossways in the fish's gullet. The Fish King choked and died. Nanaboozhoo fed its carcass to the birds and the animals. The bear ate the most. He guzzled down gallons of fish oil and grew so fat that afterwards he had to sleep all winter just to thin down a bit. To this very day, his body is layered with heavy fat, the source of bear-grease.[20]

In 1890, the U.S. Fisheries Division of the Eleventh U.S. Census sent Bert Fesler down the shore from Duluth all the way to Isle Royale to collect fishery data for the Census Bureau.[21] He made the trip with two other men in a rented boat and kept a careful diary, noting the settlements along the way. Fesler listed the names of the fishermen in the order of the location where he encountered them. He recorded Beargrease among the fishermen of Grand Marais and Good Harbor Bay.[22]

Rough weather held Fesler down for a day at Grand Marais, and in his diary entry he mentions the names of a few prominent locals, records a shopping list from Mayhew's trading post and jots down a few comments on the local Indians. John Beargrease was probably one of the half-breeds he mentions:

> Held at Grand Marais by the weather until 5:30 p.m. Entertained in the interim by young Mayhew, who had been in the Signal Corps and is a bright young fellow; by Jos. Scott, the frontiersman; by Swank, the fisherman; by Adolph Karlsen, who owns an interest in a silver mine a few miles back which he hopes will make him a millionaire some day, and by Indians, half-breeds, etc... As with all Indians we have seen, they work for a living and are law-abiding citizens. The Indian of the books is not this Indian.[23]

In the days of John Beargrease, fishing was a way of life for everyone along the shore. Beargrease would have employed a combination of traditional Anishinabe fishing techniques and modern techniques learned from the Scandinavians. As a mail carrier accustomed to the summer rowboat route, he knew the shorelines between Two Harbors and Grand Marais as well as, if not better, than any fisherman on the shore. He also knew all the fishermen. He knew their favorite spots. He knew their techniques.

A fishing operation could usually use a good boatman, particularly one who knew the lake as well as Beargrease. A strong back helped with the labor. A sizable catch of fish had to be quickly cleaned, salted, iced and packed. The locals harvested lake ice in the winter primarily for icing down fish in the summer. Successfully fishing the lake meant year-round work.

Fesler wrote about the fisherman of that day saying, "Some fished from a fixed location, but most of them during those years were itinerant and had lifted nets at various places between Duluth and Isle Royale."[24] Beargrease would have been among the itinerant, following the fish wherever they might lead.

Beargrease's mail customers relied heavily on fishing. The Redmyers, the Tofte brothers, the Nelsons at Lutsen and most of the settlers along the shore made their primary living from the fishing industry. They braved the waters of Lake Superior in small fishing skiffs no larger than his mail boat.

Beargrease did not make a career out of fishing. Unless a man was catching and selling a large volume of fish, it was an impractical way to make a living. The packing companies that carried the fish to market often charged fisherman steep freight rates.[25] That alone kept profit margins small. Beargrease made better money by carrying mail.

Dockworker and Day Laborer

When John Beargrease was not running a trap-line, hunting deer or bear, guiding pioneers to their claims, fishing Lake Superior or carrying the mail, he apparently found some employment in Two Harbors working the docks. The enormous docks at Two Harbors were specially constructed piers from which railcars loaded with iron ore could dump their contents into large hoppers which in turn filled the cargo holds of gigantic ore ships. At the height of the operation, the piers at Two Harbors were offloading 10,000 tons of ore in six hours. Hundreds of men called "ore punchers" worked at dizzying heights above the water to offload the cars. Armed with long iron poles, the ore punchers had to manually pry loose the sticky iron ore from the cars and encourage it to dump into the hoppers. It was a dangerous vocation.

The Two Harbors newspaper routinely reported horrific accidents and deaths. Men often lost their footing and fell from those great heights or found their limbs trapped in equipment, sometimes crushed or severed. More than one ore puncher was himself suddenly dumped into the hoppers along with iron ore he was prying loose. In the winter, the moist ore froze solid in the cars and needed to be steamed free. "Through the years, the memory of large plumes of steam rising from the railyard and the dock became an indelible part of the colder months of life in Two Harbors."[26] The steam, of course, added to the hazards.

According to historian Anna Anderhagen, John found work on those docks as an ore puncher. Ore punching was a source of labor always available for anyone willing to risk their neck for a pittance. Regular dock workers were making a lucrative $1.65 a day by 1899,[27] but the average day laborer could be hired for considerably less.

Like most of the Indians of Beaver Bay, John Beargrease is listed on the census records as a day-laborer. This meant he was willing to take work wherever it might be available. One day, it might mean working on the docks in Two Harbors; another day, it might mean working in a lumber camp, and on another day, it might mean doing county road work.

Back to the Mail Route

While Beargrease was off the mail trail, other carriers named John were running his winter route. In the fall of the year that John Beargrease and George Hogobone threw up their mail contract, the *Two Harbors Iron Port* reported that the *Dixon's* summer mail contract would expire for the year on November 1, after which a new party would take over the winter and overland route.[28] John Koss of Two Harbors and John Peck were that new party. They served the route in John Beargrease's absence, but they had a hard time of it. While Koss and Peck had the route, the Grand Marais newspaper often complained of late deliveries. Heavy storms hampered them. Unusually deep snows in the winter of 1893 (too deep even for dog team) forced Koss and Peck to row the entire distance against inclement weather and rough waters more than once. The *Cook County Herald* reported the difficulties:

> The mail from Two Harbors was two days late this week on account of the heavy storm on the lake. (*Cook County Herald*, Nov 25, 1893)

> On account of the ice and rough weather on the lake the mail from Two Harbors which was due here Tuesday noon did not arrive until 5 O'Clock Thursday evening. Although considerably fatigued by the day's travel, mail carrier Peck started back after a rest of but a couple of hours, intending to row all night. (*Cook County Herald*, December 16, 1893)

After one or two seasons on the route, Koss and Peck were finished, but they were only subcontractors. The star route contract for the winter mail line was actually in the hands of a bidder named Mr. Mott, and as the winter of 1894-1895 was approaching, Mr. Mott was looking for a new subcontractor. He found a man from the Grand Marais end of the route to take over, but it was not John Beargrease.[29] Beargrease was no longer interested in subcontracting. Instead, he wanted the star route contract for himself.

In September of 1894, Chris Murphy, the new Grand Marais Postmaster and editor of the Cook County Herald received a document from the U.S. Postal Service soliciting bids for the star route. He reported that "the Postmaster General has issued a circular inviting proposals for carrying of the United States mails from July 1st, 1895 to June 30th, 1899. Contracts will be let for both the star and steamboat routes from Two Harbors to Grand Marais and the route from Grand Marais to Grand Portage."[30] Murphy, who was a friend of Beargrease, may have helped him write a bid and submit it to the Postal Service (since Beargrease was illiterate). On January 5, 1895, Murphy reported that John Beargrease had won the bid for the winter route from Two Harbors to Grand Marais and would be paid $728.00 a year.

CHAPTER EIGHT

Red Charlie White Charlie

From now 'till May 15th we will receive mail from the outside world only once a week, the *Dixon's* season for carrying the mail having expired the 31st [of October]. As in former years the mail will be carried in rowboat from Two Harbors so long as the lake remains open, after which time it will be carried over the trail by dog train. (*Cook County Herald*, November 2, 1895)

Beginning November of 1895, Beargrease was back on the mail route. He had not carried the mail to Grand Marais since the summer of 1891, and in his absence a lot had changed. The mail trail had seen significant improvement; a lumber camp at the Cross River was now receiving mail through Lutsen, and a Norwegian settlement at Carlton Peak had sprung into existence. Though the community did not yet have a post office or even an official name when Beargrease began his 1895 mail runs, he now carried items in his mailbag addressed for names like Engelsen and Tofte.

Tofte

In 1893, the Norwegian immigrants Hans Engelsen, his brother Torger, his wife Johanna and her twin brothers John and Andrew Tofte arrived on the North Shore. Hans Engelsen was an experienced Scandinavian sailor who had also served with the U.S. Navy. They set to work clearing land near Carlton Peak, some two miles beyond the mouth of the Temperance River. They raised several small cabins and began carving a community out of the wilderness. Hans Engelsen worked with the Tofte twins at logging and boat building, but he also found a niche in county politics and quickly took office as the Cook County Commissioner.

More Norwegian settlers joined the little community in 1894, and a year later permanent homes replaced the cabins. Locals referred to the new settlement as Carlton Peak. Hans Engelsen applied for a post office in 1896. In his application to the Postal Service, he proposed that the town be called Carlton, but that name was already taken by another Minnesota town. Hans resubmitted his application with the name Tofte, the name of the farming and fishing community back in Norway from which many of the Carlton Peak settlers originally hailed. In November of 1897, the *Cook County Herald* announced:

> The United States government has conferred a great honor upon another of Cook County's citizens. This time it is our worthy county commissioner, Hans Engelson. He has been appointed custodian of public moneys, licker of stamps and reader of postal cards at the post office to be established at his home of Carlton Peak. The name of the new post office will be "Tufte." (*Cook County Herald*, November 13, 1897)

Even though the Tofte Post Office was a late addition to the North Shore Mail Route, it became an important station for John Beargrease in the last years of his mail run. Chris Tormondson, one of the early Tofte settlers, later recalled, "Tofte was one of his regular stopping places and he always stayed at my Uncle Hans Engelsen's boarding house."[1] A fine photo of Hans Engelsen and Andrew Tofte posing in front of the Tofte Post Office has survived. Hans holds a dip net over one shoulder and cigar stub in the other hand.

Schroeder

Other things had changed since Beargrease last ran the mail. Mail bound for his stop at Redmyer was now laden with letters and parcels for the men of the Schroeder Lumber Company at the Cross River. The Schroeder Lumber Company began their formal assault on the great forests of the North Shore in 1895. They opened a logging camp to take down thirty-six miles of white pine stands along the Cross River. They built a series of impounding dams, stop dams and sheers back to the head waters of the Cross River. The loggers hauled logs by horse teams to the river and then sent them downstream in a series of plunging, artificial floods created by the dam systems.

For six years, the hundreds of men employed by the Schroeder Lumber

Company depended on the post office at Lutsen for their mail delivery. Their presence on the trail added significant weight to the mail bags. In 1901, the Schroeder camp received their own post office. The city of Schroeder at Cross River remains to this day.

Beargrease Boys in Grand Marais

During Beargrease's absence from the route, county crews had cut and widened a section of the mail trail from the Cook County line at Caribou Point all the way to the Lutsen bridge. By the time Beargrease returned to the mail route, the trail had begun to resemble a road.

In Grand Marais, a new postmaster had taken over. Chris Murphy, the new owner and editor of the local newspaper, had acquired the office of postmaster from Henry Mayhew. Murphy moved the post office from Mayhew's multipurpose trading post to the Howenstein building on the west side of town, out of which he was also publishing the *Cook County Herald*. Murphy alerted the community to the arrival of the weekly mail by hoisting the American flag above the Howenstein building as soon as the mail carrier came.[2]

One month after reporting to the public that the *Dixon's* summer contract had expired for the year and winter mail service had begun once again, Chris Murphy was singing the praises of John Beargrease and his brothers:

> As mail carriers, those Beargrease boys, who have the contract from Two Harbors to Grand Marais, are world beaters. So far, they have arrived here ahead of time every trip. Kagiget, who carried the mail last trip, left Beaver Bay Sunday noon and arrived here at eight o'clock Monday morning, making the sixty miles in the incredible short time of twenty hours and arriving here twenty-eight hours ahead of time. He came in a rowboat and delivered mail to two post offices on the way." (*Cook County Herald*, November 30, 1895)

In 1895, the two post offices between Beaver Bay and Grand Marais were Redmyer and Lutsen. The post office at Tofte would be added to the route within two years. Kagiget [Gageget], the mighty rower, was John's nineteen-year-old half-brother. As the star route contract holder, Beargrease could afford to employ his brothers to make the mail run for him. The Beargrease mail team of John, Joe, Peter and Gageget kept the mail coming for the next four winters.

The winter of 1895 was mild. The lake shore did not freeze, and shipping was still running in January. John and his brothers probably carried the mail by rowboat for much of the season. The *Dixon* began its regular ferries up and down the shore in April of that year but, by contract, could not start carrying the mail until the winter term expired a few weeks later. On May 15, Beargrease and his brothers had to relinquish the mail to the *Dixon* until fall.

Lost in the Fog

In the fall of 1896, John and his brothers were back at it again. As Beargrease headed out on the mail route in late October, his wife Louise was headed into the final month of her latest pregnancy. On November 24, 1896, a new life was born into the Beargrease home. It was a girl. They named her Mabel Louise. Less than two weeks after baby Mabel entered the world, her uncle Peter almost left the world.

On Monday, December 7, John's brother Peter Beargrease and A. H. Wegner, the Beaver Bay postmaster and Lake County Commissioner, set off from Beaver Bay in a rowboat on their way to Two Harbors. As county commissioner, Mr. Wegner frequently had business to attend to in the county seat and was known for hitching an occasional ride with the mail carrier.[3] Peter would have been going to retrieve the mail from Two Harbors before making his way back down the shore with it. The cold air temperature and relatively warmer lake water, however, combined to create a thick, heavy fog in which the two boatmen lost their way.

For two nightmarish days and two black nights, they wandered about in the heavy fog, unable to see the shore, unable to see the sky, unable to get any sense of direction. Though both men were experienced boat handlers and navigators, the lake had played a cruel, blinding trick which left them little hope of survival. They had not brought any food with them. The bitter cold and soaking mist froze them to the bone. Postmaster Wegner lost his strength, nearly dead, leaving Peter, with his fingers frozen to the oars to handle the boat alone. Peter was eventually able to find the way in and land them a few miles down the shore from Beaver Bay. Famished, frozen and feverish, the two men barely managed to drag themselves to help.[4]

A Painful Injury

It was an unlucky year for John Beargrease. A month and a half later, while running along behind the dog team in the darkness, Beargrease gashed his head on the point of a sharpened tree limb protruding over the trail. A county crew had cut the branch in preparation for the winter mail service, but they had left the dangerous protrusion:

> John Beargrease, the mailcarrier sustained a very painful injury on Monday evening while on his way here from Two Harbors. The evening had grown dark and John was running behind his dog team when a little this side of Pork Bay, he ran against the limb of a tree, which projected over the trail, cutting a deep gash in the top of his head. Part of the limb had been cut off, leaving a sharp point, which came in contact with his head. With the blood streaming down his face he proceeded to Cross River where he had the wound dressed, and continued his journey the next morning. (*Cook County Herald*, January 16, 1897)

Bloodied and stained, Beargrease came tumbling into the midst of the Schroeder Lumber camp where he found concerned friends to bandage the wound and offer him lodging for the night. The next morning he hitched the dogs to the sled, and he and the mail were on the way again.

For the next several weeks after taking a gash in the head, Beargrease continued to chase the dogsled down the mail trail and back, waiting impatiently for ice to form along the shore. Even in winters when the temperatures are cold enough to freeze the shore line, the water often does not freeze up until mid-February. As of February 6, ice had still not formed along the shore to ease the flow of the mail. Snow fell every week that winter, but the temperatures remained mild. Near the end of February Minnesota's frigid winter temperatures finally prevailed and froze the shoreline, allowing Beargrease and his dogs a considerably easier trip to Grand Marais and back. That spring, the *Dixon* was still waiting for the ice to break up in mid-April.[5]

As he had done the previous spring, Beargrease held the mail contract until his season ended on May 15 even though the *Dixon* was already making her runs.[6] Those last weeks of the route were the worst. The lake was rough enough to make the rowboat an undesirable option. The snow, if any was left, was soggy and rotten. The trail turned to slippery mud and slush, and all the streams and rivers became engorged with melt off. Just before mid-May and Beargrease's last week on the mail route that season, the weather held another surprise. Heavy snow blanketed the North Shore.

The North Shore Road

John and his brother Joseph along with much of the population of the

North Shore spent time during the summer of 1897 working on the North Shore road. For the day-laborers in those communities, road work provided a welcome source of employment. Almost everyone in town participated.

All along the line, county crews transformed the mail trail into an actual road. In Cook County, the entire distance between the Lake County line at Caribou Point and Grand Marais was under improvement. "Every river and creek is provided with a good substantial wagon bridge and the road is fit for travel at any season of the year," the *Cook County Herald* boasted that fall.[7] Chris Murphy, the editor of the *Herald*, claimed that the Cook County section of trail was a "splendid piece of road" fit for horse and buggy, but he complained that the Lake County road between Beaver Bay and the Cook County line remained unfinished. He announced that Cook County would be bringing pressure on the Lake County officials to finish their section of the road so that a stage route could be opened between Two Harbors and Grand Marais.[8]

The Lake County government was more concerned with the thirty-two mile span of road that connected Two Harbors and Beaver Bay than they were with the road between Beaver Bay and Cook County. Prior to the summer of 1897, only eleven miles of the trail to Two Harbors had been upgraded to resemble a road. That summer, settlers and local laborers completed the remaining twenty-one miles. Lake County officials intentionally employed local labor in an effort to "keep the money at home as much as possible."[9] The Lake County Financial Statement for the fiscal year ending January 2, 1898, shows payments of $122.00 to John Beargrease from the road and bridge fund. The same financial statement shows that John's brother Joseph made $192.00 working on the road that year. The Beargrease brothers must have known that the road they were building would one day bring an end to the days of mail by dogsled.

Selling the Dogs?

While the road work was still underway in August, a startling rumor reached the newspapers. Word was that Beargrease sold his famous dog team for $150.00 to a group from Duluth who were reported to have "left last week for the Alaskan gold fields."[10] As the gold rush in Alaska was reaching its full swing, the newspapers reported that "Dogs for the Klondike are being gathered in all large cities."[11] Would he have really sold his dogs? It seemed unthinkable. How was the mail to be delivered that winter?

When Beargrease made a trip to Two Harbors in late August, the editor of the *Two Harbors Iron News* asked him about the sale of his dogs. The next day, he reported to his readers that the story of John Beargrease selling his dogs was merely an unfounded rumor. John had not sold his dogs, nor had he even entertained the idea:

> John Beargrease was in town yesterday. When questioned as to selling his dog team to Duluth parties going to the Klondike, he stated that he had never even had a proposition from residents of that or any other place to dispose of them. (*Two Harbors Iron News*, August 20, 1897)

A Difficult Start

On November 6, 1897, Beargrease set out on his first mail trip of the season. As he set off in the rowboat, the Two Harbors newspaper took note of the trip and paid him high praise:

> John Beargrease is again carrying the mail on the winter route between Two Harbors and Grand Marais, he having arrived on his first trip last Saturday. With the exception of a few years John has had this contract since the routes establishment, and there is probably no more [reliable] carrier in the land, there are but few harder routes. (*Two Harbors Iron News*, November 12, 1897)

November of 1897 was cold and storm ridden. An early November storm with strong headwinds covered the ships with ice. The disagreeable weather persisted through the month, forcing Beargrease to fight freezing temperatures and tossing waves as he rowed the route back and forth. A late November storm brought wind so strong that the residents of Grand Marais claimed "it never blew harder there." While preparing to leave Grand Marais harbor, the rudder on the steamer *Dixon* froze stiff.[12] For all that cold and misery, though, no snow had fallen yet. The rowboat was still Beargrease's best option.

The cold, high winds persisted into December. "The thermometers registered 7 degrees below 0 this morning and the wind from the southwest was a corker,"[13] the papers read. Thankfully for Beargrease, December also brought enough snow to begin using the dog team, but just when it seemed he might settle in for the regular sled runs, the cold weather broke with a sudden thaw. "The soft weather of yesterday was disastrous to sleighing," the *Iron Trade Journal* reported on December 23. The warmer temperatures only lasted a day, just long enough to ruin the snow. The next day, the temperature plunged well below zero again, but that was all just weather in Minnesota.

Gun Trap

In addition to bringing the mail, the mail carrier brought the latest news. In January of 1898, John Beargrease and his dog team came sliding into Grand Marais with the mail and a horrifying story. Pete Olsen of Tofte had perched a shotgun in the woods with a tripwire strung across a deer trail and attached to the trigger. His wife protested, fearful that a passing neighbor might trip the wire and be killed. Mr. Olsen assured her that he would set the trap where no one would hazard upon it. The following morning when he went to check the trap, he somehow managed to become tangled in his own tripwire. When he did not return, his wife asked Hans Engelsen of Tofte and Hedley Redmyer to conduct a search. They followed his tracks in the snow and were shocked to find his corpse, clearly shot to death. Completely unaware of the gun trap, Hedley circled around the corpse, looking for the tracks of an assailant. In so doing, he triggered a second tripwire which would have unloaded the shotgun's second barrel had the gun not jammed. The two men were dumbfounded to discover the loaded gun aimed directly at them some sixteen feet from where they stood.[14] As the *Two Harbors Iron News* stated it, "In a case of this kind sympathy is meager. A man who sets a gun in the woods is an enemy to all his fellows who might go that way."[15]

> John Beargreace [sic], the mail carrier, says that the practice of putting out 'set guns' and setting bear traps where people walk into them is carried on to such an extent in Lake county that the Indians are afraid to go into the woods. (*Cook County Herald*, January 8, 1898)

Pony Express

As Beargrease fought the weather, struggling with his dog team along the new section of road between Two Harbors and Beaver Bay, it occurred to him that the new bridges and the road improvements made it possible to run a horse on that stretch of the trail. All he needed was a horse. By the end of the year, he had acquired one. The Two Harbors newspaper took note of the new road, Beargrease's new horse and the inevitable obsolescence of the dog team:

The new county road knocks out considerable of the novelty of the North Shore mail route, as John Beargrease will relegate the dogs and hereafter drive a horse. The dogs will be retained, however, on that portion of the route between Beaver Bay and Grand Marais. John's dogs have made the route known all over the country, but must give way to the advance of civilization by good roads. Within a very few years a weekly stage will cover the route between here and Grand Marais. (*Two Harbors Iron News*, December 31, 1897)

Beargrease used the horse to pull a sleigh of mail from Two Harbors to Beaver Bay. At Beaver Bay, he stabled his horse and transferred the mail to the dog team for the rest of the run to Grand Marais and back. Upon arriving in Beaver Bay again, he unhitched the dogs and harnessed the horse that would take him the rest of the way into Two Harbors. It was a terrific improvement in speed and convenience, and Beargrease immediately began wondering about taking the horse the whole distance.

The twenty-four miles from Beaver Bay to the Cook County line was still rough trail with lots of dips, narrow passes and inadequate bridges. Could it be done? He would need something more durable than a toboggan or sleigh. Within a week or two of making his first mail run with the horse, he had formulated a plan.

In early January of 1898, John Beargrease stopped in at the Iron Range Boiler Shop in Two Harbors for a conversation with Foreman Moses. Beargrease described the type of operation he had in mind, and Moses set to work drawing up plans for a heavy-duty steel toboggan. It was eight-feet long, three-feet wide and one-foot high and weighed 360 pounds. Three steel ribs ran along the bottom to keep the toboggan from sliding laterally on the ice. "It is thought that Beargrease intends to haul some freight as well as the mail. His new rig will easily carry a ton," the *Two Harbors Iron Trade Journal* reported.[16]

As the newspapers speculated, Beargrease intended to carry extra cargo on his runs to Grand Marais and back. A winter freight delivery would be a great accommodation for the people of Grand Marais and extra revenue for Beargrease. The innovative steel toboggan was finished by February of 1898, but we do not know when he first placed the new rig into service.

Charlie Horses

In order to pull the heavy 360-pound toboggan bearing mail, freight and a driver, Beargrease needed a second horse. Willis Raff explains,

"Depending on the amount of mail and freight and trail conditions, the toboggan was pulled by one or two horses, hitched to either single-trees or double-trees."[17] Local lore remembers that he hitched two horses to the toboggan. One was a bay, the other was white. Beargrease named the horses Red Charlie and White Charlie. In his beautifully illustrated *Tales of the Old North Shore*, Howard Sivertson speculates that Beargrease may have reminiscently named the horses after the schooner *Charley* on which he and his father had served decades earlier.[18] Beargrease intended to use Red Charlie and White Charlie for delivering mail and freight up and down the shore just as the schooner *Charley* had delivered mail and freight in years past.

Beargrease was already well-known among the North Shore settlers for shouting orders to his dog team in Ojibwe. He became equally well-known for shouting at his horses. Apparently, the horses understood Ojibwe too. "Many of the old timers remember well how John Beargrease could be heard yelling at his horses, long before he reached the Beaver Bay Post office."[19]

The winter of 1897-1898 turned out to be a disappointment. Low precipitation and warm temperatures made the toboggan impractical for much of the season. Thin ice formed on the bays by early February, but ships were still coming and going from Grand Marais, and the *Cook County Herald* speculated that the *Dixon* might start her runs in March.

The warm spring temperatures also made the steel toboggan impractical, and for a brief while, Beargrease tried hitching his new team to a wagon. John Slater of Beaver Bay once accompanied Beargrease on an attempted wagon run. His niece, Elizabeth Garrison, narrated the story:

> Uncle John [Slater] told about going on the route with Beargrease to learn the route. He had a team of horses and a small wagon so he could deliver things to people on the way. They got to the Manitou [River] and it had been raining and in that red clay it was slippery. They tried to get up the hill but the horses and wagon would slide back down, so they tried to go back the way they had come and the same thing happened there. Uncle John said this old Beargrease had the most colorful language you ever heard in your life, in fact Uncle John learned quite a bit that he could use later himself.[20]

It was on an occasion like this that Beargrease ended up abandoning a sack of mail.

The Spanish-American War Incident

In mid-February of 1898, Beargrease left the media mail sack hanging in a tree at the Cascade River. He showed up in Grand Marais with only the letter mail, leaving the townsfolk completely ignorant of the bombing of the battleship *Maine* which triggered the Spanish-American War. In a 1953 taped interview, Van Johnson, a Grand Marais resident, tells the story in his own words:

> During the winter months at that time the mail was carried by John Beargrease of Beaver Bay. I remember the time that the warship Maine was blown up, and on that trip with the mail John got too much out of a bottle (he was on a little toot) and then hung the paper sack mail in a tree at Cascade River; it was two weeks before we really got word about the Spanish War.[21]

Why did Beargrease leave the mailbag in the tree? And why did it take two weeks before they saw the papers? According to another version of the tale, "Beargrease explained he just got a little tired at Cascade and hung the mail pouch containing the [newspapers] on a tree. He promised to bring them on his next trip…" But when he trekked into town the next week "Beargrease gave the gathering crowd a sheepish grin and explained that he had simply forgotten to pick up the pouch from the tree at Cascade… [thus] Beargrease was responsible for the people in Grand Marais being the last Americans to learn that war had been declared."[22]

It was a tough spring. Perhaps it was the mild weather, or perhaps, as Raff suggests, Beargrease was simply suffering the terrible effects of too much cheap rum the night before with Hans Engelsen and the Tofte twins.[23]

The Spanish-American War incident was not the only time this sort of thing happened. A month later, the *Cook County Herald* complained that "the mail carrier from Two Harbors was two days late in arriving here this week. With the exception of a very few papers, he brought only the letter mail, leaving the balance on the way."[24]

The weather was not cooperating, and the mail load, particularly the media mail, was getting heavier and heavier. In mid-March of 1898, the lake was still impassable. Between Beaver Bay and Two Harbors, heavy northeast seas prevailed. On the Grand Marais end of the trail, a gliding mass of soft, floating icebergs made mail by sail impossible. If Beargrease was attempting the dogsled, the rapid melting forced him to abandon the team and carry the mail the rest of the way on his back, or at least lighten the team's load.

The Half-Breed Dog Puncher

Within a few days of this second mail-mishap, a delegation of three Cook County officials set out for Two Harbors by dog team: Treasurer Charles Johnson, Register of Deeds C. H. Carhart and County Commissioner Hans Engleson. "We had not a boat suitable to make the whole trip by water, so we took an Indian and dogs and went over the mail route," Johnson said. They traveled by dog team as far as Beaver Bay. From Beaver Bay, they risked high seas in a boat to Two Harbors. Apparently, it was a harrowing voyage. "One of the party… has since told me privately that a dog train is good enough for him at this time of the year and that when I am going afloat in a washtub again to count him out," Johnson said. The men were on a mission to petition the Lake County government to complete the twenty-four miles of unfinished road between Beaver Bay and the Cook County line. Johnson told the newspaper:

> If this road were made, the winter trip between Two Harbors and Grand Marais, eighty-nine miles, can be made by stage in two days' time. At present we are dependent upon the primitive dog team and half-breed dog puncher. Everybody who has ever had anything to do with such an outfit knows how exasperating and ineffective is this mode of communication with distant points. (*Cook County Herald*, April 9, 1898)

Of course, John Beargrease was the half-breed dog puncher to which Johnson referred, and despite the pressure of the Cook County officials, the Lake County government did not get around to completing that last twenty-four miles of road for another year.

The *Dixon* resumed her weekly service on April 1, but as usual Beargrease retained the mail route until the winter contract expired in mid-May:

> The Dixon will resume mail carrying May 15th, Beargrease taking his summer vacation at that time. (*Two Harbors Iron News*, April 22, 1898)

During his "summer vacation," Beargrease was troubled by Louise's failing eye-sight. He brought her to the doctor in Two Harbors where she was diagnosed with cataracts.[25] The Beargrease family received some financial assistance from the county that year. In 1899, John and Joseph

Beargrease both appeared in the Lake County Financial Statement for the previous year as having received disbursements from the poor fund: Joseph Beargrease [who had no dependents] received $8.00 for the year. John Beargrease received $20.00 for the year.

Windfalls

For the first three weeks of November, 1898, the North Shore newspapers were reporting fine and fair weather, "purely of the Indian summer variety." Then, on November 24, the first blast of winter cut loose with a regular northwest blizzard. The snow fell and the winds raged for twenty-four hours. When it was all over, the trains were blocked by great drifts, the city streets were filled with snow, and two steamers were run aground: one at Beaver Bay and one at Baptism River.[26]

Fortunately for Beargrease, he was not on the mail route during the storm. Unlike in previous years, he was not yet running the mail. Instead, the *Dixon's* season had been extended so that she would carry the mail through November and pick up the route as soon as the lake was navigable in the spring. The new arrangements pleased the folks in Grand Marais, but it effectively cut two months off of Beargrease's income:

> The last trip of the season for the Dixon is scheduled for tonight. She will clear from here about midnight. John Beargrease will resume carrying of the North Shore mail tomorrow on his winter contract. (*Two Harbors Iron News*, December 2, 1898)

On Saturday December 3 Beargrease set off from Two Harbors. The heavy snow combined with numerous windfalls from the storm impeded his progress. It took him four-and-a-half days to fight his way down the shore. If he was driving the dog team, he found the difficulties of the trail bad enough but nothing with which he was unfamiliar after twenty years on the trail. If he had Red Charlie and White Charlie, Beargrease would have found himself cursing the day he decided to use horses in the snow. The horses would tire quickly in such deep snow, and the numerous windfalls would require him to unhitch and re-hitch the team frequently as he maneuvered them through the woods.

He did not arrive in Grand Marais until Wednesday. The local paper reported, "The old reliable winter mail line made its first trip on Wednesday. John reports the roads the worst he ever encountered."[27] In order to be back in Two Harbors by Saturday, he had to turn around immediately and face those same roads, the same deep snow and fresh windfalls all the way back.

Beargrease's hopes of using Red Charlie and White Charlie and the steel toboggan would have to wait until trail conditions improved. The trail did not improve. On his first mail run of January, even though he was still using the dogs, he had such a great struggle with the fallen trees blocking the trail that he was forced to once again abandon the media mail on the trail. Even so, he did not arrive in Grand Marais until Wednesday evening. The next day, Grand Marais resident Catherine Kirby Jones wrote in her diary, "Letters came late last night but the papers are still behind on account of wind falls on the route."[28]

Lubricated Wheels

Despite the difficulties, the overland trail remained the only option. The lake was far too rough. That January, Louis Engelson and John Tofte decided to challenge Lake Superior's January gales and make a winter fishing run. The *Cook County Herald* reported, "They lost 800 pounds of fish and came near losing themselves; when they reached the shore they were so nearly frozen that they could not open the door of the house."[29] When Beargrease arrived in Tofte that same week by way of dog team, he could easily empathize with his friends' tale of their narrow escape. He himself had been in the same boat on more than one occasion. A few rounds of rum after that was only appropriate.

The people further down the shore did not offer John much sympathy. The residents of Hovland complained, "No newspapers were received in the mail of last week, much to the disappointment of many. It has been suggested that the carriers at the west end of the route lubricate their 'wheels' with something more reliable."[30] By that, they meant to infer that Beargrease had carelessly abandoned the mail sack because he had been drinking again. They still had not forgiven him for the Spanish-American War incident of the previous spring. It may be true that Beargrease was drinking. Given the circumstances of his occupation, it would have been unreasonable to remain sober.

It was not the drink that impeded his ability to get the entire load of mail through that week. The North Shore residents did not appreciate how difficult it had become for the southwest-end mail carrier to move the enormous loads of mail that the seven hundred residents and uncounted lumberjacks of Cook County expected each week. Beargrease planned on picking up the abandoned mail sack the following week, but he would need help because the following week had its own regular load of mail.

Beargrease enlisted one of his brothers—probably Joseph—to assist. They hitched up a few more dogs to form two dog teams, one carrying the media mail and one carrying letters. When they reached the location at which John had abandoned the sack, they took it on too, redistributing the load between the two teams. In her diary, Catherine Kirby Jones noted, "The mail arrived Wednesday noon and required two teams of three dogs each—last week's paper mail made the extra load."[31]

A Cold Snap

Beargrease was disappointed that the trail conditions prevented him from using his expensive team of horses and the steel toboggan. In late January, the weather began to promise improvement. Temperatures plunged. As he and the dogs set out from Beaver Bay Sunday morning, January 29, temperatures were already well below zero. By that evening, they had fallen to thirty-two below. By morning, the temperature had dropped another ten degrees. By Tuesday morning, the mercury had fallen to more than fifty below zero. At such extremes, it was no longer safe to run the dogs, and Beargrease had to take shelter somewhere along the trail. He ended up staying somewhere like Lutsen, waiting for the temperature to rise enough that he could finish the trip safely.

A cold mail carrier and four cold dogs slid into Grand Marais a day late.[32] The *Two Harbors Iron Trade Journal* remarked, "If your paper is late this week, just bear in mind that the ink is frozen as hard as a piece of pig iron..."[33]

Despite the delay and the inevitable frostbite, the low temperatures worked in Beargrease's favor. Ice formed quickly along the shore, and by February 10, it was already over a foot thick. A week later, the *Cook County Herald* reported that the Lake was "completely covered with ice as far as the eye could see, no rising vapor being visible anywhere."[34]

> Two years ago the weather was moderate and it snowed every week. This winter it is colder than blazes, but don't snow... If mercury don't soon climb a little higher, we will be forced to admit that it is slightly chilly on the North Shore. (*Two Harbors Iron News*, February 10, 1899)

At last, Beargrease was able to hitch up Red Charlie and White Charlie, take them on the lake ice and easily glide over the route. He arrived at Tofte in record time. He was so far ahead of schedule, he decided to celebrate with the Tofte boys a bit. He celebrated a bit too much. The *Cook County Herald* that week coyly read, "John Tofte brought the mail from Tofte this week, the regular mail carrier having 'played out' at his place."[35] Beargrease recovered quickly.

Flu Season and Cold Remedies

During the rest of February and March, the ice remained solid and safe, but the weather continued to vex the mail delivery. The last week of February brought a heavy blizzard which pinned Beargrease and his horses down somewhere along the route. In Grand Marais, the newspaper said, "Heavy snowstorm delayed the mail from Two Harbors a day and a half this week."[36]

Despite the snow, Beargrease continued to run his horse team on the ice, saving time and effort and giving his poor dogs a well-deserved rest. "Beargrease reports ice good all the way to Two Islands," the papers read in March.[37]

A few weeks later, though, Beargrease was a day late with the mail. This time, it was not the trail, the weather or even too much celebrating with the Tofte boys. The *Cook County Herald*, with its incessant obsession with the winter mail delivery, reported, "Beargrease arrived on Wednesday afternoon with the mail; a case of grippe caused the delay,"[38] which is just to say that he was down with the flu. The invincible John Beargrease was mortal after all.

According to Edward Greeve, Beargrease had his own home remedy for colds and influenza. He claims that Beargrease drank a bit of kerosene to cure a cold.[39] Apparently, the kerosene cure worked because the next week the mail "was sharp on time..."[40]

Meltdown

Red Charlie and White Charlie were still charging up and down the frozen lake into April that year. One newspaper speculated that the ice in certain places might be thirty feet thick.[41] Nevertheless, the ice could not last. The April temperatures rose as dramatically as the January and February temperatures had plunged. When Beargrease arrived in Grand Marais with the mail that first week in April, he could only report solid ice from "Beaver Point to Duluth."[42]

On April 8, he and his brother Joe set off from Two Harbors with the Charlie-horses. Joe was along to help with the extra freight that John was carrying on this run. As they made their way along the shore, they noted how warm winds were already disintegrating the ice. With the combined weight of sleigh, mail and freight, the horses were pulling more than two tons over the soft, slushy ice. Progress was slow. By the time they reached Beaver Bay, John realized that the ice was no longer safe.

He faced a sticky situation. The ice was rotting. Snow was fast melting off the trail, but even if the snow were fresh, the dogs could not pull the heavy load. As a last resort, he and Joe stabled the horses and loaded the rowboat. The Beargrease brothers dragged the mail boat across the frozen harbor of Beaver Bay and dropped it into the cold April waters, chancing the April seas and dodging shifting ice floes as they went. They arrived in Grand Marais on Wednesday, and Joe told Catherine Kirby Jones and her son Kirby all about the adventure. Catherine wrote in her diary, "Mail thirty hours late. They came with horse and sleigh from Two Harbors to Beaver Bay on the ice with a ton and a half load. The rest of the way in boat."[43] As John and Joe returned by boat on Thursday morning, they were caught in the first thunderstorm of the year.

Two weeks later on Wednesday, April 26, Catherine wrote in her diary, "Mail came at 6 a.m. The last trip John Beargrease will make this spring." Not only was it the last trip that spring, it was the last time John Beargrease would ever carry the mail as the star route contract holder.

Finishing the Road

Lake County finally got around to finishing the road between Beaver Bay and the Cook County line that summer. For its part, Cook County went to work improving the so-called road on its side of the line.

Beargrease's star route contract with the Postal Service expired, and the U.S. Postmaster was soliciting new bids. This year, however, the Postal Service assumed that the road between Two Harbors and Grand Marais would be completed and passable by larger passenger sleighs drawn by teams of horses. Beargrease did not have the capital to invest in the equipment. As far as we know, he did not even bother attempting to make a bid. The Ambrose A. Call Mail Co., a firm out of Iowa, won the bid for the new star route. They, in turn, auctioned the route to the cheapest subcontractor. In August, even before the road was completed, the *Two Harbors Iron News* announced the new mail carrier would be Peter Black of Two Harbors:

> The awarding of this contract marks the time of the retirement of the dog train which for years has carried the North Shore mail, and the inauguration of a semi-weekly winter mail and stage line. Mr. Black is already making his preparations for carrying out the contract. As the travel promises to be exceptionally large the coming winter, he will put on a first class stage line, and afford every facility for handling this traffic comfortably. (*Two Harbors Iron News*, August 25, 1899)

Mr. Black's "first class stage line" consisted of a passenger sleigh delivering mail twice a week. He divided the route into three relays: the first team driving from Two Harbors to Beaver Bay, the second team from Beaver Bay to Pork Bay and the third from Pork Bay to Grand Marais. The mail was to leave Two Harbors every Tuesday and Saturday at nine in the morning and arrive at Grand Marais on Thursdays and Mondays.[44] That was assuming there was snow enough on the road for the sleigh to run.

That September, while the road work was being completed, the Lake County Board members hired John Beargrease to shuttle them up and down the shore in his rowboat so they could check on the progress at various points along the road. When he submitted a request for $10.00 of compensation for his time and the use of his boat, the Lake County Commissioners meeting disallowed the expense.[45]

Lake County crews finally completed the road on time for the winter mail route, and the *Two Harbors Iron News* offered a long tribute to the North Shore road, its history and the Beargrease brothers who carried the mail on it. It was the end of an era. For the historical perspective it provides, the article is reprinted here in full:

> The most valuable improvement of years to the business interests of the North Shore was completed this week. We refer to the new county road from Beaver Bay to Grand Marais, constructed by the joint action of the public-spirited commissioners in the Counties of Lake and Cook. By the opening of this piece [of] road, a wagon road from Two Harbors to Grand Marais, a distance of 85 miles, is provided, and it is also the securing of a long desired outlet by the citizens of Cook county, and the settlers at intermediate points along the route. It is essentially a winter road at present, but while passable in summer during

the dry weathers, it will probably be little used. When navigation is open it is more expeditious and profitable to patronize the boats.

The work of previous years had provided a good road to about six miles beyond Beaver Bay settlement, where the extension this fall was begun. The distance from the point of beginning to the Cook county line is about 23 miles, and from there to Grand Marais about nine miles, making nearly 32 miles of new road. It is located well back from the lake, north of the hills, and is of easy grade. There are miles as level as a floor. The bridges over Baptism and Manitou rivers are substantial and durable structures, and all culverts and short bridges are put in with a view to safety and durability. The Baptism river bridge is 100 feet long. It has always been a cherished desire to build the county road along the shore of the lake the entire distance, but the impracticability of such a route, because [of the topography] of the shores, was manifest. It would cost as much as the county is worth. Its greatest distance from the shore is about six miles.

There are twenty lumber camps between Two Harbors and Grand Marais. In the past it has been necessary to send all supplies down in the fall by boat. It was also essential to figure to a nicety the rations, clothing and other supplies for the men and animals, because when winter shut down, there was no communication with the outside world except over rough trails on snowshoes, and any supplies brought in would have to be packed, a method too laborious and slow to be thought of. Now tote teams can reach Two Harbors from any point, and the round trip can be made in a few days.

The importance to Two Harbors business-interests of the new road will soon be realized. All supplies sent in during the winter months will be transferred here. Men and teams en route to and from camps will secure a portion of their supplies from our dealers. For ten years lumbering will be a great industry along the shore, and thousands of dollars will flow into our hotels and business houses.

The road in one way strikingly presents the onward flow of civilization. For the first time in the history of the North Shore the United States mail will be carried the entire distance between Two Harbors and Grand Marais by team. For the thirty or more years that the mail route has been established, dog teams in charge of Indians have been employed in the service. The route was one of the hardest in the United States, but a very commendable degree of regularity was maintained. No matter what the weather or conditions, the mail generally reached here every Saturday. The Beargrease boys have made the weekly trip up and down the line, and suffered hardship almost beyond human endurance. Through drifts and blizzards they have fought their way, and in the spring plodded through mud or waded through freshets. For a few weeks during some winter's have had ice on the lake the entire distance, but it was an exception. Two mails per week, which the new contract calls for, will bring the folks who are opening up that country, nearer than ever to civilization. (*Two Harbors Iron News*, November 17, 1899)

For John Beargrease, the "hardship almost beyond human endurance" was over, but new hardships lay ahead.

Wigwam on Beaver River peninsula, circa 1875. (Courtesy Bay Area Historical Society)

Wigwams at Beaver Bay, circa 1875. (Courtesy Minnesota Historical Society)

Beaver Bay in 1870 as depicted by Mrs. J. J. Lowry. The schooner *Charley* can be seen coming to dock at the mouth of the Beaver River. Four wigwams are visible on the Beaver River Peninsula. (Courtesy Bay Area Historical Society)

Left to Right: Augusta (Constance), John, Joseph, Charlotte, Louise and Mary Ann Beargrease, circa 1895. (Courtesy Cook County Historical Society)

John Beargrease with his daughter Mary Ann, circa 1897. (Courtesy Cook County Historical Society)

Ojibwe woman, spuriously identified as Mrs. John Beargrease, with child in *tikinagan*. (Courtesy Cook County Historical Society)

Beargrease brothers on the mail trail with the dog train. (Courtesy Bay Area Historical society)

John Beargrease
on the mail trail
with the dog train.
(Courtesy Bay
Area Historical
Society)

John Beargrease on the mail trail with the dog train. (Courtesy Bay Area Historical Society)

North Shore mail carrier (often misidentified as John Beargrease) with dog team. (Courtesy Bay Area Historical Society)

Beaver Bay Wieland-Wegner store, hotel and post office with distinctive cupola. Beaver Bay girls posing in front include Mary Ann Beargrease. (Courtesy Bay Area Historical Society)

Steamer *Dixon* docked at Grand Marais.

John Beargrease with rifle. (Courtesy Cook County Historical Society)

John Beargrease with rifle. (Courtesy Cook County Historical Society)

John Beargrease's steel toboggan. (Bay Area Historical Society)

Augusta (Constance) Beargrease-Lemier and Mary Ann Beargrease, 1908.

John Lemier, Augusta (Constance) Beargrease-Lemier, and son Cyrus Lemier.

Mary Ann Beargrease with her son Clarence William Hangartner Beargrease, grandson of John Beargrease, circa 1920. (Courtesy of Cook County Historical Society)

Nancy Beargrease, the last survivor of the Beargrease chidren.

CHAPTER NINE

Old John

In the last decade of his life, John Beargrease was known to the hunters and trappers of the North Shore as "Old John." Old John's last years were full of joys—more children, the marriage of two of his daughters, the birth of grandchildren—but they were also years of trouble and hardship for the whole Beargrease family. The loss of the mail route created financial hardship. Two of Beargrease's siblings struggled with mental illness. A legal battle over land holding and a broken heart threatened one daughter. Frequent sicknesses, the death of his mother and the deaths of more children cast a growing shadow over Old John Beargrease and his family.

To alleviate the financial blow of losing the mail route, Beargrease liquidated some assets including the timber rights for a land claim of his near the head of the Palisade Creek. The Palisade Creek is a stony little waterway that weaves back and forth through the hills behind Silver Bay before it finally empties into Lake Superior at the foot of Palisade Head. Beargrease sold the timber rights for five hundred dollars.[1]

The sale could not have been without at least a tug of reluctance. Beargrease had seen land left behind by the timber industry all up and down the North Shore. The once proud and tall stands of pine were fast disappearing. Beargrease needed the money, though. In October, 1899, the same month he sold the timber, Louise gave birth to another son. They named him John George. The baby died a month later.

A Beaver Bay Sensation

The same week that his son died, John Beargrease's sister Mrs. Bluesky was arrested for allegedly attempting to kill her husband. Mrs. Bluesky, one of the daughters of Chief Moquabimetem, was married to Frank Bluesky of Beaver Bay. The *Two Harbors Iron News* called it a "Beaver Bay Sensation."

Dr. Budd and Probate Judge Hannon of Two Harbors traveled to Beaver Bay to examine the woman's sanity. They found the people of the village divided over the affair. Some said she was insane; others claimed she was not. The Indians avoided her, and none would remain with her in the absence of a custodian. When Dr. Budd and Judge Hannon questioned them about the situation, they would only respond, "I don't know." The investigation was further hampered in that Mrs. Bluesky had never learned English, and no one offered to translate for her.[2]

Mrs. Bluesky was transferred to Grand Marais, where she could be examined by the Cook County Sheriff. A week later, the Sheriff and his wife escorted her to Fergus Falls where she was committed to the State Hospital on December 3, 1899.

The first notes on her file from the Fergus Falls State Hospital case book reads, "[Subject] is an Indian Squaw and does not speak English. She is quiet, lies in bed peacefully and quiet—no trouble, smiles when addressed and says a few words in the Indian language."[3] No Ojibwe interpreter was immediately available in the hospital, but three days after she was admitted, Mr. Hannon, the Lake County Judge of Probate, arrived. He told the staff what he had learned about the case by means of an interpreter. Apparently, (whether delusional or not the judge did not know) Mrs. Bluesky believed that her husband had illegitimately fathered their grandson. The notes from her case file say, "that patient's daughter had had a child and that patient accused her husband of being the father, that she had endeavored on several occasions to take his life." The horror of the allegation accounts for the reticence on the part of the family to speak to outsiders. The staff at Fergus Falls diagnosed her as manic depressive, suffering from a hereditary disorder.

Being locked in a State Hospital with no one who speaks your language might drive anyone to the brink of insanity. In the case notes, her moods fluctuate from cheerful to violent. Explosive episodes landed her in restraints again and again over the first two months of her commitment.

After February, however, the madness seemed to pass. She took a job in the laundry and began to learn English. Thirteen months after her hospitalization, she seemed completely sane. The January 1, 1901, case notes say, "Several letters have been sent to her people asking them to come and see her." Her brother Peter Beargrease did come see her, but unfortunately not under the best circumstances.

Peter and the Devil

John's younger brother Peter had married Louise's sister Cecile. In November of 1896, their first and only child was born. They named him Peter Jr. Like his brother John, Peter Sr. had a penchant toward alcohol, but unlike his brother John, the drink got the better of him. Peter was arrested while drunk for destruction of property and threatening violence.

On March 7, 1901, he too was committed to the Fergus Falls State Hospital. Peter's occupation is recorded as a "packer in the woods." His personal history reads, "Attended school but five days. Is as intemperate as possible." In addition to alcohol problems, Peter wrestled with severe delusions. The case notes tell his story: "Says if he sees people with a light he will kill them, but if without a light he will not ... has ungovernable passions." The case notes from the day of his admission paint a troubling picture:

> ...makes many absurd statements, as he can run 1,000 miles a day, that he drank 10 gallons of milk for breakfast, but on close inquiry it was learned that these statements are made from his lack of knowledge of distance and measure. Gives history of intemperance, was intoxicated about two weeks ago, and admits that when intoxicated he loses control of himself and becomes very ugly and violent. Has for the past three days seen angels and heard them singing, the devil has also come to him as a big black man and has told him that he would kill him, but patient is not much afraid as he believes himself to be the stronger. Also since being at the hospital has seen God and heard Him whisper to him, will not tell what was said. For the past two weeks has also felt greatly depressed because his wife, angry at his intemperance and lazy habits, drove him from home; since then has thought of taking his life and says he would do so now were the opportunity given. Memory is somewhat impaired...[4]

The next day, however, Peter had recovered his wits. The case book entry for March 8, 1901, reports, "Is quiet and remains in bed very well. Is somewhat dull and sleeps the greater part of the time. Answers all questions by replying, 'You bet.' Has seen no angels nor the devil since admission and has not heard God's voice today."

A week after admission, he was allowed to visit his sister Mrs. Bluesky. The case book says, "Seemed very much pleased to see her and made the statement that he had come to the hospital with the intention of taking her home, said he was not insane upon admission and that he had just taken a little too much whiskey."

By mid-April, he was very eager to return home and expressed fear that his wife might not be getting enough to eat or even that she might leave him for another man while he was gone. On April 18, the hospital discharged both Peter and Mrs. Bluesky. They traveled home together to Beaver Bay.

In their absence, the community had been ravaged by small pox. The Anishinabe families, and the Bluesky home in particular, were hard hit:

> The Two Harbors health officers report two or three cases of small pox in Blue Sky's family at Beaver Bay. They are said to be of the worst form. Care should be taken that no one from Beaver Bay is permitted to come here. (*Cook County Herald*, March 16, 1901)

> Peter Beargrease and Mrs. Blue Sky have been released from the insane asylum at Fergus Falls. They returned to Beaver Bay last week. Mrs. Blue Sky was formerly a resident of the county and Peter Beargrease used to carry the mail along the north shore. (*Cook County Herald*, May 4, 1901)

Though declared cured and released, both Peter and Mrs. Bluesky found themselves returning to the hospital in later years. Peter was committed and released four times over the ensuing fifteen years.

Charlotte Beargrease Decker

In Beaver Bay, John Beargrease was adjusting to life without the mail route, and dealing with family issues. His family survived the Beaver Bay small pox epidemic. In April of 1901, just three weeks before his brother and sister were released from Fergus Falls, his wife Louise gave birth to a strong, healthy son. They named him George.

Other family matters were pressing in on the Beargrease home too. Their oldest daughter Charlotte had fallen in love. Charlotte was a seamstress for the Beaver Bay Indian community.[5] The Indian seamstress caught the eye of Herbert R. Decker, a young man from Two Harbors. All of the Beargrease daughters were beautiful, and John and Louise must have known it was only a matter of time before the suitors would be coming for them.

The nervous young Herbert Decker called on the Beargrease home in Beaver Bay to court their eighteen-year-old daughter. Mary and Augusta must have been awash with the excitement. Louise and John would have felt that customary bewilderment as they realized that their daughter had become a woman and, moreover, they were about to receive a white man for a son-in-law.

Charlotte and Herbert were married in a Catholic wedding ceremony on March 14, 1903. Charlotte settled in Castle Danger with her husband. On December 6, 1905, Old John Beargrease became a grandfather when his daughter gave birth to her first child, Angeline Louise Decker.

A Story from Tofte

As Beargrease wandered the North Shore, he remained a welcome guest all along his old mail route. In October of 1902, a large contingent of Norwegian settlers arrived at the Tofte community. Among them was fourteen-year-old Chris Tormondson, who encountered John Beargrease while living with his uncle, Hans Engelsen. In his memoir, he tells the story:

> One night, while I was still living with my uncle, Beargrease came in on his sled after supper was over. He hadn't eaten so Mrs. Engelsen set a meal before him at the table. As he ate, he would sneak pieces of meat from his plate into his shirt. When he left the table, I followed him outside. He went to the shed where his dogs were bedded down for the night. There he removed the pieces of meat and gave a few to each dog. I told Mrs. Engelsen about this and she gave me a big pan full of meat scraps. When I took it out to Beargrease, he grinned from ear to ear, and gave the dogs a good meal. A quarter of beef cost only 3 cents in those days, and my aunt figured there was no sense in letting the dogs go out on the trail hungry.[6]

The Sonju Family

Other Norwegian settlers remembered stories about Beargrease too. In 1903, Andrew and Karoline Sonju arrived in Lake County with their family. The Sonju's had four children, the oldest of which was a daughter named Elise. In 1975, Elise used a tape recorder to record her memoirs. Her granddaughter typed them into an unpublished manuscript entitled, *Homesteading on the North Shore*.

According to Elise's recollections, the Sonju family's first introduction to Beargrease occurred while they were still living in an abandoned lumber camp at Little Marais:

> The way we first met John Beargrease in October, 1905 at Little Marais: my
> mother had seen a canoe, or boat, with John Beargrease and a little old lady, his
> mother, from up on the beach at Little Marais. So a few days or a week later,
> we saw smoke on top of the hill. It was raining in October, so my mother said,
> "Those Indians are up there under the trees." She had seen them up there while
> she was out getting the cow. So my mother was boiling potatoes for dinner and
> she took two hot potatoes, wrapped them up in her apron, and we four kids
> trailing behind her, went up the hill to see John Beargrease sitting under one
> tree, his mother under another tree, in a drizzly rain, with a little fire in front of
> them. My mother handed John Beargrease the hot potatoes. He felt them and
> he said, "Dinnertime." That was our first acquaintance with John Beargrease,
> and the beginning of a good friendship.[7]

Nancy

The same year that the Sonjus first met John Beargrease, he became a
father again. It was 1905, and Louise gave birth to a daughter. They named
her Francis, but in later years she went by Nancy.

Nancy is also the English name that Beargrease's mother Newigagamibig (Otoe) had taken. By 1905, his mother was advanced in years. The
1905 census lists her as eighty years old, living with John and Louise in the
Beargrease home under the name Nancy. Davis writes, "John's mother Otoe,
old and wrinkled but always friendly [made her home] with John."[8]

Several months after first meeting the Norwegian family from Little
Marais, John Beargrease and Newigagamibig returned to the Sonju home
as they were passing through the area. The image of Beargrease with his
aged mother in the canoe and camping in the woods brings to mind the
many stories of the traveling companions Nanaboozhoo and his grandmother Nokomis. Elise Sonju remembered John and Nancy spending the
night with them in the winter of 1906:

> John Beargrease and his mother came back to our place in Little Marais where
> we were living in a little house. We had moved out of the [lumber] camp at
> that time because it was so cold. They stayed at our home, sleeping on the floor
> because we only had two rooms. In the morning at 4 o'clock there was a little
> old Indian lady sitting in the middle of the floor, lacing her moccasins. We had
> a hired man, Ole Thorad from Norway, who sat and looked at her. He said, "I
> believe that woman must be crazy." He didn't realize what Indians were like.

Medicine Man

North Shore resident Charles Christensen told an even more peculiar story about an encounter with John Beargrease. Charles was the son of Louis P. Christensen, who worked with law enforcement in Two Harbors. "John was a medicine man," Christensen claimed and offered this anecdote from his own boyhood as evidence:

> When I was young boy, about 7 years old, I was suffering from warts—good, plain every-day warts, but instead of one or two warts, both my hands were covered with them.
>
> The warts over the knuckles and finger joints were especially painful, as they would bleed every time I would flex a hand muscle. The local doctor tried every known method to eliminate these warts, but of no avail.
>
> An aunt of mine, who used to teach school at Castle Danger, would come to Two Harbors over the week ends, when possible. There were not roads to this community at that time, but a boat would bring in supplies or passengers ever other week. However, about one mile west of Castle Danger, was a trail used by John Beargrease on his mail deliveries. My aunt took this trail and decided to walk to Two Harbors. While walking this trail, she met John Beargrease, whom she knew real well. During the course of the conversation, she told him about my warts. John told her to bring me down to the Lake in Two Harbors on a certain date. The exact date was important, as the position of the moon was necessary, in performances of Indian rites.
>
> We presented ourselves as instructed, and I remember John Beargrease pulling a small buckskin sack from under his shirt. From this sack he extracted a handful of some gray powder, which he then sprinkled around me. I was told not to move outside of this circle. He then started a chant, and after some more dust sprinkling, he bowed to the moon.
>
> He then told me, "You go home now. Do not use any other medicine for three weeks." I went home, and three weeks later, all my warts had disappeared, leaving no scars. After 71 years from that day, I am still free from warts. The local doctors were amazed.[9]

It is reasonable to suppose that Beargrease inherited a vast wealth of traditional Anishinabe medicine practices. Christensen related this story in 1977. If he was correct in his recollection, the incident must have occurred in 1906. It is interesting to note that, even in those early days, the old mail trail was already closely associated with John Beargrease. All along the shore, any stretches of the trail that had not been absorbed by the new roadwork came to be called the John Beargrease Trail.

Hunting at Maple

Meanwhile, the Sonju family had relocated to their claim six miles west of Little Marais to the community of Maple, a small community in Crystal Bay Township. Maple was not a real town but just a few settlers within walking distance of each other. Beargrease continued to call on the family. Elise recalled that John often came and hunted on their land, sharing the spoils with the family:

> He would come hunting up on the homestead when we moved back there, with his dog team. His son Joe was with him most of the time, a young teenager. One time he brought his whole family; they always stayed at our house all night. When he got a deer, he always gave us part of it. One time he came up with his gun; he had no bullets, so he asked my mother if she had some .22 bullets. My mother happened to have two bullets. He took my mother's .22 pistol (my mother was a good shot), went out in the woods, brought home a deer. It was snowing heavily. They brought the deer in the house and skinned it right on the floor in front of my bed, where I was ill with a stomach ache. I'll never forget the smell of that raw meat from that deer in front of the bed. [10]

Though Elise felt nauseous, the Sonju family was grateful for John's generosity. Beargrease, in turn, was grateful for permission to hunt on their land. Everyone in the Sonju family appreciated the Beargreases except for Topsy, the family dog. Every time John and his dog team came up the road toward the Sonju residence, Topsy would sense their approach from a distance and start to growl. Topsy never did make peace with the Indian or the Indian dogs. Karoline Sonju used to tease the dog even when Beargrease was not around. Elise recalled that her mother would only have to say, "Beargrease, Beargrease!" and the paranoid Topsy would raise his hackles and start to growl apprehensively.

Mary's Claim

The Sonjus were not the only family making homesteads in the woods of Lake County. In the spring of 1906, a new township of government land was opened for settlement. John Beargrease, who knew the surrounding land better than anyone, moved quickly on behalf of his twenty-one-year-old daughter Mary. She filed the paperwork and paid $100.00 to a professional locator for settlement on a valuable 160-acre tract of land at the head of the Beaver River. The tract she selected was three miles from what is now known as Cloquet Lake, about fifteen miles by way of the Beaver River from Beaver Bay.[11]

During the spring of 1907, Mary had a fourteen-foot by sixteen-foot cabin built on the land, and by July she had moved into her new home. It was a "comfortable habitation at all seasons, and suitably furnished with necessary articles of household and kitchen furniture."[12] She cleared about an acre of the land and planted crops. Mary lived alone except for the company of a single dog, but she frequently went to-and-fro between Beaver Bay and her homestead on various errands and to check the mail. When she came to town, she had a group of friends with whom she spent time in Beaver Bay and at Lax Lake. These friends included Julia Wood, the editor of the *Lax Lake County Advocate.*

Lax Lake

The Beaver Bay area was undergoing aggressive logging and, along with it, experiencing some aggressive growth at Lax Lake, a small lakeside community a few miles outside of Beaver Bay. A. DeLacy Wood, the previous founder and editor of the *Grand Marais Pioneer* (and forty-seven other newspapers he started in the course of his life) had moved to the shores of Lax Lake in 1903 and begun publishing a paper called the *Lax Lake County Advocate.* It was essentially a local paper for the Beaver Bay residents. A. DeLacy Wood dreamed of seeing Lax Lake develop into a town in its own right. Every issue of the *Advocate* boldly proclaimed "the new town of Lax Lake." After a few years, DeLacy relocated to start another newspaper in Two Harbors, but he left the *Lax Lake County Advocate* in the capable hands of his daughter Julia.

Julia was operating the paper in 1907 when the Alger-Smith Lumber Company put in a railroad to Lax Lake in order to facilitate the timber harvest. The lumber company operated by hauling logs from the surrounding area and laying them up on the frozen surface of Lax Lake. "Old timers talk of being able to walk across the whole lake on logs."[13] Throughout the summer, a hoisting crew lifted the logs from the surface of the lake and loaded them onto the flat beds of waiting lumber trains. It was massive operation.

The lumber industry made A. DeLacy Wood's dreams come true. The tiny community of Lax Lake blossomed into a boom town. "There was a barber shop, steam laundry, steam bath house, steam bakery, lodging house, blacksmith shop and two saloons."[14] In addition, Lax Lake had its own post office, its own newspaper and plenty of illegal liquor operations. It seemed that Lax Lake had completely eclipsed nearby Beaver Bay, but Lax Lake depended solely on the lumber company. When the timber ran out, the Alger-Smith company removed their operation and pulled out their railroad, eventually even taking the rails. The town quickly dwindled back to just a few settlers living on a ghost-town lake shore, bereft of trees.

Julia Wood saw the writing on the wall as early as 1907 while the lumber industry was still in full swing. In an editorial entitled "The Great Pine Forests Are Fast Passing Away," she lamented, "The old settler and casual observer now sees more clearly than ever that it is only a question of time, and not far distant either, when the great pine forest on the North Shore of Lake superior will be a thing of the past, and the grandeur and solemnity of the vast Lake superior region will to a great extent be decreased …"[15]

Julia was a personal friend of the Beargrease family and a close friend of Mary Beargrease. Because of her interest in the Beargrease family, news of their affairs featured regularly in her newspapers. Julia's running comments on the family's ailments and accomplishments, comings and goings, allows us an intimate glimpse into the Beargrease home. Unfortunately, the first four years of the newspaper have been lost to time. The Minnesota Historical Society Library has a single roll of microfilm which preserves the years 1907 through 1909.[16]

Augusta's Wedding and Mary's Illness

In the spring of 1907, the Beargrease girls were eagerly anticipating Augusta's wedding. Augusta Beargrease, who had recently changed her name to Constance, had fallen in love with John Lemier, a French-Canadian (perhaps Ojibwe) residing at Grand Portage. She had met him while staying in Grand Marais the previous summer.

Augusta planned to marry Mr. Lemier in Duluth at the end of April. As the wedding day approached, though, she fell sick with fever.[17] Mary was sick too. As her condition worsened, she left her homestead to come home where the family could care for her.[18]

The wedding day drew closer. Augusta recovered quickly, but Mary's condition proved to be mumps. The family brought her to the hospital at Two Harbors. On April 27, Mary remained confined in the Two Harbors hospital while Augusta and her fiancé were married in Duluth. John

Lemier returned to Grand Marais the next day without his new bride.[19] Augusta traveled only as far as Two Harbors. She stayed there to help nurse her sister back to health.

Mary spent several weeks in recovery.[20] By the end of May she had recuperated enough to be discharged. On Saturday, May 25, John Beargrease traveled to Two Harbors to accompany her back home,[21] and Augusta left for Grand Marais where she and her husband took an apartment together.[22]

By early June Mary was fully back on her feet and even made a trip to Duluth.[23] Mary's grandmother Nancy was not faring so well, however. The June 1 edition reported, "The aged mother of John Beargrease is still in a very critical condition and is not expected to last long." The same edition of the paper reported that Louise's father, "Alex Boyer, the old settler of Beaver Bay has been laid up the past week with rheumatism and is not able to leave his bed." Alex (Giggity) Boyer improved that summer, but Nancy did not. She died a week later on June 11. Julia Wood reported, "The aged mother of John Beargrease died Tuesday morning at Beaver Bay."[24]

Alert Indian Guide

At the time, that his mother Nancy died, Beargrease was working as a guide for a settler named Mr. Douglas and his cousin Carl Smith. They had a fine claim twelve miles from Lax Lake on Stony River but needed a guide to get them to the claim and back. The *Advocate* reported that they returned to Lax Lake for provisions "accompanied by their faithful Indian guide who knows the shortest and best route through the big forest of Lake County."[25] It was fortunate for their faithful Indian guide that they returned when they did. It allowed him to be home to attend to his mother at the time of her passing. His new employers waited in Lax Lake several days for Beargrease to finish with his sad business. On Friday of that week, he accompanied the settlers as they headed back for their claim.[26]

With Mr. Douglas securely located on his claim, Beargrease was looking for work again. He joined up with Sam Sproat, a local Beaver Bay land-locator-surveyor-explorer-prospector-woodsman. Like most of the settlers in those days, Sam and John had notions of striking it rich in prospecting. In the July 27 edition, Julia Wood reported, "Sam Sproat and John Beargrease of Beaver Bay were in town this week and left on Friday last on a prospecting trip through the new towns and will be absent about ten days." The "new towns" were small, hopeful start-ups like Maple and Finland. Most of them never actually became towns, but after the boom at Lax Lake, anything seemed possible. Beargrease stopped in at Mary's homestead that week to ensure that everything was in order during her absence. Beargrease and Sproat did not strike gold. A week later they were back in town to escort three more settlers to a backwoods claim.[27]

Later that summer Mary was ready to return to her claim. She had been absent since falling ill in April. Julia Wood wrote, "Miss Mary Beargrease arrived in town Friday and proceeded to her claim in one of the new towns."[28]

Late summer on the North Shore is berry season. In mid-August, Julia Wood observed, "Many of the people of Beaver Bay have been absent the past week on a blueberry picking excursion down the North Shore."[29] A week later, she wrote, "John Beargrease, the alert Indian guide, returned from a trip in the woods this week." He returned to accompany his family on an excursion to the iron range to pick berries.

While the family was away, "Miss Mary Beargrease made a flying trip from her homestead to Beaver Bay."[30] Mary hoped to find the family at home, but alas, they were gone berry picking. Mary did, however, find her grandfather Giggity Boyer in a terrible state. His rheumatism had become so acute that he could not move from his bed, and he had to be treated at the Budd Hospital in Two Harbors.[31] When Beargrease returned the next week, he traveled to Two Harbors to bring his father-in-law back to Beaver Bay.

It was at that time that John and Louise decided to move in with Boyer. He owned a large home in Beaver Bay. Under the same roof, they could care for him as they had done for John's mother. The 1910 Federal Census shows Alex (Giggity) Boyer as the head of household, living with the Beargrease family.[32]

Delivering the Mail Again

John Beargrease lost his star route, mail-carrying contract in 1899, but in less than a decade he found his way back into the mail carrying business, at least on a limited basis. In 1908, his younger brother Joseph had been hired to carry mail on John's old route from Two Harbors to Grand Marais. This meant driving a stage when there was sufficient snow cover, but when there was no snow on the ground, it meant using a horse and cart or just a pack horse. Joe sometimes resorted to the old method of carrying mail by sail, or, according to the Duluth newspaper, mail delivery by canoe. So long as the lake was accommodating, the rowboat was preferable to slogging along the muddy road and over swollen, flooding streams with a horse. Then again, the lake can never be trusted, especially in the off-season. According to the *Duluth News Tribune*, "Joe Beargrease is famous for having survived an eight day storm on the lake in a canoe, while carrying mail from Two Harbors to Grand Marais. He was given up as dead, but surprised the settlers by rowing in on the eighth day and landing safe and sound."[33]

The same *News Tribune* article which mentioned Joe's eight-day canoe adventure refers to John as "deputy for his brother, Joe Beargrease, United States mail carrier for settlers up along the North Shore." He must have taken the of the mail-stage team at least occasionally. On November 20, 1907, he was issued a citation in Lake County for "driving over a bridge faster than a walk" and was fined $10.00.[34]

Royal Indian Blood

Shortly after the new year of 1908, Beargrease and his younger brother Joseph made a trip to Duluth. While attending to their errands in Duluth, they decided to sample a few of the local refreshments and became a bit too refreshed. In an article entitled "Noble Indian Escapes Wrath of the Law," the *Duluth News Tribune* reported that John and Joe were arrested and charged with being drunken and disorderly. The *News Tribune* said "[John Beargrease] pleaded guilty to a charge of drunkenness yesterday in municipal court and was fined $3 and costs."[35] The ruling was quickly overturned when local friends of Beargrease rose to his defense, entering testimony regarding his character and reputation. The paper went on to say, "Later on, the good character of this lineal descendant of royal Indian blood was established and his sentence was suspended. The Beargrease brothers are descendants of a former Chief of the Chippewa tribe."

Charlotte's Illness

Not long after John and Joe returned from their embarrassing adventure in Duluth, Charlotte fell ill. In February, the *Lake County Advocate* reported, "Mrs. Charlotte Decker of Beaver Bay, who has been quite ill for some time was taken to the hospital at Two Harbors last week where it is hoped she will soon recover… Mrs. John Beargrease went to Two Harbors Thursday to see her daughter, who is very ill, in the hospital at that place."[36] Charlotte was released from the hospital a few weeks later but did not fully recover.

In March, the Beaver Bay Anishinabe population left for their annual trip to the sugar bush. The family was in the sugar bush near Grand Marais when word reached them that Charlotte's health was failing again. Beargrease's dog team pulled him in to Little Marais where he was able to catch the train down the shore to Two Harbors.[37] The urgency of his mission demanded more speed than even his legendary dogs could provide him. We do not know if he arrived on time to bid his daughter farewell:

> The funeral of Mrs. Charlotte Decker occurred at the Catholic Church at Two Harbors on Sunday last, Father Pett officiating. The remains were taken to Beaver Bay on Monday and interred in the Catholic Cemetery at that place. The deceased leaves a husband and a two year old girl to mourn her loss. (*Lake County Advocate, April 11, 1908*)

Indian Girl's Land

In July of 1908, a fellow by the name of Martin Steinman took an interest in Mary Beargrease. He was not interested in matrimony, but in her land at the head of the Beaver River. He filed an affidavit with the land office, trying to prove that Mary was not in compliance with the settlement laws. He hoped to force her off the claim so that he could lay hold of the land. In the affidavit, he stated that Mary had never maintained a residence on the land, but resided instead with her family at Beaver Bay. He claimed that her filing was fraudulent in that she was an Indian ward of the U.S. government, drawing annuities, and therefore was not entitled to make a homestead entry.

By December 21, the Duluth Land Office was ready to hear the case. In an article sympathetic to Mary's cause and entitled, "Indian Girl's Land," the *Two Harbors Iron News* related the details of the case. The article reported, "The land Miss Beargrease has homesteaded is said to be one of the most valuable tracts in the Beaver Bay region. The case was hotly contested and many witnesses were heard. The decision will not be made known for some time."[38]

Steinman seems to uniquely embody the constant injustice that American Indians suffered at the hands of white land-grabbers. Whether Martin

Steinman or the U.S. Government, the impetus was the same. Like U.S. Government policies toward Indian treaties and native peoples, Steinman was not above playing dirty to get what he wanted. He apparently tried to frighten Ms. Beargrease off the land by burning her cabin to the ground. A Duluth newspaper picked up the story:

> The little cabin owned by Mary Ann Beargrease on her claim near Beaver Bay burned down one night last month while Miss Beargrease was visiting her father in Beaver Bay. Mystery surrounds the burning. The cabin was unoccupied at the time of the fire and Miss Beargrease is at a loss to understand how the fire started.
>
> Miss Beargrease is the daughter of John Beargrease, known to the hunters and trappers of the North Shore as "Old John." The family is one of the best known of Indian families of the north. They have lived on the North Shore of Lake Superior all their lives and the whole family was in town about two months ago to testify in the land case of Martin Steinman, who is trying to get the Indian woman's claim away from her on the grounds that she has never made it her home. The case is still unsettled.
>
> Miss Beargrease was in town this morning on business connected with her case.
>
> "Yes," she said, "There are some people on the North Shore who have fought my right to my claim, but I had no idea that they would go so far as to burn my little cabin. I don't know whether anyone set fire to it or not, but it all seems very queer. There was not fire in the forests and I cannot think of a single way the house could have caught fire, unless someone took the trouble to start it.
>
> "I will go back in the spring and build it again. I have a gun and a little dog and I am not afraid in the least."
>
> Miss Beargrease lived most of the time alone in her cabin. The nearest neighbor was nearly a mile away. She says that she was never afraid. On the contrary, she says she enjoys the life and is looking forward to the springtime so that she can get to work on the new cabin.[39]

Steinman failed to frighten Mary off the land, and he failed to force her off through legal channels as well. The document of the Decision of Register and Receiver in the Martin Steinmann vs. Mary Ann Beargrease case records some of the testimony entered by the defendant. Ms. Beargrease testified that she was born and raised in Beaver Bay and attended the public school. She stated that for three years prior to her land entry, she was employed as a domestic servant with a Beaver Bay family.[40] Her father John testified that he had been a registered voter for the last twenty years and was currently "in the employ of the United States Government in the capacity of mail carrier." The document goes on to detail Mary's occupation of the land, the occasions of her absence, her development of the land, and to dismiss the charge that she was receiving annuities.

Mary's case was settled, but not until August of 1909. In the meantime, Mary was preoccupied with other matters.

Mary and Willie

In October 1908, Mary and Augusta Beargrease took a trip to Duluth together.[41] Perhaps it was while they were in Duluth that they visited a studio to have their photograph taken. The photo still survives. While on the trip, Mary would have filled her sister in on the details of her budding romance with a local boy from Beaver Bay: young Willie Hangartner.

The Hangartners were an old, well-established Beaver Bay family. The Swiss-born Jacob Hangartner originally settled in Beaver Bay in 1861. Six years, later Jacob married Elizabeth Zimmerman who bore him nine children. Elizabeth originally came to Beaver Bay with her family when she was only nine years old. After a few years, though, the Zimmerman family and several other Beaver Bay families abandoned their claims and traveled by ox cart to the German colony of New Ulm. Unfortunately, New Ulm was the wrong place to be at that time. Little Elizabeth saw her father and two of her brothers killed while the family attempted to flee the violence of the infamous Minnesota Sioux uprising. A Sioux chief struck down her father before her eyes. Her brothers were shot while trying to escape. Her mother died shortly after the massacre, and the surviving Zimmerman children returned to live with relatives on the North Shore. Elizabeth married Jacob Hangartner in 1867. Needless to say, Elizabeth harbored no love for Indians.[42]

Mary Lornston, the childhood friend of Beargrease girls had married John Hangartner, one of the Jacob and Elizabeth's sons in July of 1908. John Hangartner had a younger brother named Willie, "a tall man… with deep brown eyes and liked by everyone."[43] Together with several of the other young people of Beaver Bay and Lax Lake, Mary and Willie attended local social events. The Lake County Advocate kept tabs on the comings and goings of the area's young adults, and Mary Beargrease can be seen in the locals column in the company of Wille Hangartner.[44] The Beaver Bay young people occasionally traveled to Two Harbors together, but they did not have to travel all the way to Two Harbors to find fun. The Betzler family, the largest family in Beaver Bay (twenty-one children), was always throwing dances for the locals.

Saturday night dances provided regular amusement for the North Shore settlers. The dances were virtually the only entertainment available between Two Harbors and Grand Marais. Different families hosted the dances in their homes from week to week. The accounts of the early settlers describe houses packed with people. They would arrive from all over. First, they would eat supper together, then out came the fiddle and the accordion. They danced late into the night.

In Beaver Bay, the Betzler family kept the community dancing. Their New Years Eve dance of 1909 even employed a dog team to keep the refreshments coming through the night.[45] Mary and Willie Hangartner attended these dances together. By the time of Betzler's big New Year's Eve dance, Mary would have realized that she was already pregnant with Willie's child. She did not tell him.

They were in love. It seemed romantic to her to imagine herself, Mary Beargrease, and her childhood friend, Mary Lornston, the two Beaver Bay Marys, soon to be related to each other as Hangartner wives. It did not seem romantic to the Hangartners. The family did not allow the match.

Apparently, Elizabeth Hangartner could not reconcile herself with the idea of her son marrying an Indian. The Hangartner parents sent Willie to sea and insured that he and Mary never met again. The February 27 *Lake County Advocate* reported, "Will Hangartner has gone to Huron, Michigan, where he will act as wheelsman on Capt. Clow's boat the coming summer." Vickie Chupurdia, a keeper of local lore says, "He wrote to her and she to him, but neither one knew that their letters were being intercepted by a relative. Mary was with child and her sweetheart didn't know. There is no record of either of them marrying and the young man grew to old age and lived alone all his life."[46] Willie Hangartner lived as a bachelor, working as a fisherman in Beaver Bay until he died in 1943. Beaver Bay resident Mary Slater recalled how old Bill Hangartner lived a lonely life but "always seemed to have a place in his heart for children."[47]

In the summer of 1909, Mary Beargrease gave birth to a son. She named him Clarence William Hangartner. So far as we know, Willie never met his son.

Finland Fourth of July

Preparations were underway that summer for a fabulous Fourth of July event at the new community of Finland on the Baptism River. The residents of Finland, Minnesota extended an invitation to all their neighbors in Lake County. They planned a display of fireworks for the evening and a national salute of one-hundred guns at sunrise. Promises of races, games, fireworks, plenty of refreshments and a big dance abounded in the *Lake County Advocate*. "The eagle will scream with no uncertain sound at Baptism River on July 4th," the Advocate hyped. It was no surprise to find Julia Wood, editor of the *Advocate*, promoting the event. Her father, A. Delacy Wood was the keynote speaker. A local Finn by the name of Joe Pelto was prepared to translate Wood's speech into Finnish.

Mary Beargrease attended the event, but she was no longer in the company of her young socialite friends from Beaver Bay and Lax Lake. Broken-hearted and shamed, she attended the event only with her ever-loyal father.

The Sonju family attended the event as well. Elise was thirteen years old by then. Sixty-six years later, she could still vividly describe the event in the sorts of details a teenage girl might notice. She described A. Delacy Wood and his two daughters, Julia and Helen: "Mr. Wood was a pompous, but nice person, a good speaker. He had his two beautiful daughters with him. They were in organdy or voile dresses, with make up on their faces; no lipstick." As she told the story, she spoke of seeing John Beargrease and his daughter Mary. She said, "John Beargrease and his daughter, Mary, were there from Beaver Bay. It was the first time I had ever seen Mary, and she was a very pretty, friendly girl, about twenty years of age."[48]

After the Finland Fourth of July, Beargrease continued to visit the Sonju family. Elise said, "The last time that I saw the Beargreases was in 1910."[49] She speculated that John Beargrease must have quit coming around for fear of game wardens in the area. Elise never heard the news that Beargrease died in 1910.

CHAPTER TEN

The Ballad of John Beargrease

Nanaboozhoo's Land

When the traders, the settlers and all types of white people came among the Ojibwe, their manner of life changed, and many things were forgotten. Some, however, still remembered Nanaboozhoo, and ten men decided to seek him out and speak with him. They fasted for many days, taking a great deal of care in preparing for the journey. They built a large, sturdy canoe of birchbark and skirted along the edge of the great lake, Kitchi Gami, paddling by day and camping on the shore by night. One night, one of the men had a dream telling him the way to the place Nanaboozhoo was living. The next day, they paddled in the direction shown him in the dream. After a long time, they saw an island. They said to each other, "That must be the place." They reached the island and pulled their canoe up on the shore. They saw his footprints on the shore leading to a beaten trail through the woods. The men followed the trail and came to a large, sturdy lodge—the home of Nanaboozhoo.[1]

Tamerak Point

By 1908, John Beargrease was occasionally carrying the mail under his brother Joseph. At that point in his life, carrying mail was only a part-time vocation which he combined with plenty of trapping and hunting and just roaming through the North Shore forests. The 1910 census lists his occupation simply as a trapper. "John Beargrease, the old mail carrier, is trapping back of Lax Lake," the *Lake County Advocate* reported,[2] but at least occasionally, the old mail carrier was carrying mail.

Beargrease's part-time return to mail carrying explains why he was back in the mail boat in 1910. Although his mail trail between Two Harbors and Beaver Bay had been replaced by a road and his dog team had been replaced by a sleigh and teams of horses, very little had changed on the route between Grand Marais and Grand Portage. The mail on that portion of the route was still being delivered by dog team in the winter and by rowboat in the spring and fall. Louis Plante, the mail carrier between Grand Marais and Grand Portage had died in 1907. His uncle and mentor, Godfrey Montferrand, was at least occasionally carrying the mail again.

In the spring of 1910, before the navigational season had opened yet, Montferrand was making a mail trip by rowboat between Grand Marais and Grand Portage. According to the popular North Shore version of the story, Beargrease was on Tamerack Point of Grand Portage when he saw Montferrand floundering in the mail boat. Beargrease leaped into the freezing water to save him,[3] a last heroic act of the great mail carrying hero. As the story goes, Beargrease saved Montferrand, but contracted pneumonia in the process.

In reality, Beargrease was already in the boat with Montferrand when they began to have trouble. They had rowed from Grand Marais to Grand Portage, delivered the mail, and were en route back up the shore when they hit choppy water. The weather was turning for the worse, and the lake was getting rough. As they rounded Tamerack Point, their little craft was caught in high, off-shore winds that sought to drive them deeper into the lake. The waves were rising. Both men knew that if they allowed the wind to push them into the lake, they would certainly be swamped.

Montferrand was taking no chances. While they were still in the shallows along the point, he leaped overboard, holding on to the rope. It was still shallow enough for him to touch the bottom. He told Beargrease to stay put in the boat while he attempted to pull them ashore. It was a risky plan. Montferrand had to fight the waves while trying to find his footing as he pulled on the rope. The boat rose and fell on the water, and the wind tried to jerk it away from him. Beargrease jumped overboard too and got behind the boat to steady it. With Montferrand pulling and Beargrease pushing on the boat from behind, the two men were able to safely land it on Tamerack Point.

Edward LaPlante, the son of mail carrier Louis Plante and a great-

THE BALLAD OF JOHN BEARGREASE   • 151 •

nephew of Montferrand, told the story in a letter he addressed to the Lake County Historical Society. LaPlante wrote, "Beargrease got pneumonia and before my uncle made another trip Beargrease was dead."[4]

Death of a Living Legend

John Beargrease might have caught pneumonia that day in the icy cold waters of Lake Superior, but it was not pneumonia that killed him. He returned sick to his home in Beaver Bay, and the May 4 edition of the *Two Harbors Iron Port Advocate* reported, "We learn John Beargrease of Beaver Bay is quite sick."

While Beargrease lay sick in bed at home, the Federal Census enumerator paid the family a visit. He found twelve occupants residing in the house. Alex (Giggity) Boyer is listed as the head of household. John and Louise and their children Joseph, Mable, George and Francis were there. In addition, Mary had left her claim, moved home and was living there with her eleven-month-old son Clarence. John's brother Peter, his wife Cecile and their thirteen-year-old son Peter Jr. are also listed under the same roof. It was a full house.

As the spring turned to summer, Beargrease's condition did not improve. Summer wore on, and his health continued to fail. By the end of June, the family brought him to Two Harbors where he was hospitalized for a week.[5] The doctor released him from the hospital because there was nothing that modern medicine could offer him. According to the *Two Harbors Iron Port Advocate*, he was suffering from "Bright's Disease," a term which suggests kidney failure. His death certificate lists "tuberculosis of the liver and meningitis" as the cause of death. John Beargrease died on Wednesday, August 10, 1910, at eight o'clock in the morning.

Beargrease's death made the front page of Delacy's *Two Harbors Iron Port Advocate*:

Veteran Mail Carrier Dies at Beaver Bay—John Beargrease Carried Mail 18 Winters

John Beargrease the veteran carrier of the North Shore who has been ill for several months with Bright's Disease died at his home in Beaver Bay last Wednesday morning at 8:00 O'clock and at the time of his death his family were all beside him.

John Beargrease was well and favorably [known] as one of the oldest Indian mail carriers on the north shore having carried the U.S. mail for 18 years by dog sleigh, sledge and pack sack, being exposed to all weather on lake and shore which no doubt had considerable to do in bringing on his premature illness.

Mr. Beargrease was a resident of Beaver Bay for the past thirty years and was a favorite among the Indians along the north shore and a highly respected citizen among the white people.

To mourn his loss Mr. Beargrease leaves a wife and five children all whom reside at home.

The funeral was held from the home of the deceased on Thursday afternoon and tenderly laid to rest in the Beaver Bay cemetery. (*Two Harbors Iron Port Advocate*, August 13, 1910)

At the time of his death, his brothers Daybosh and Skowegan, his beautiful daughters, his brave sons, his faithful wife Louise and other members of his family were all beside him to bid him farewell. How many hundreds of times had his wife and children said goodbye before as he hitched up the dogs or shoved off in the mail boat? Each harrowing journey he had made had been for their sake, and on all previous occasions, he had returned to them. This time, however, they would not hear the sound of the collar bells on his dog team heralding his homecoming, nor would they see his boat come cutting through the waves as he rounded the point of the bay.

Beaver Bay Ojibwe Cemetary

When an Anishinabe man died, they washed his body, braided his hair and dressed him in his best clothes. They buried him with his feet toward the west, for that is the direction he was to travel upon the Road of Souls. They placed a few of his personal belongings with him: a pipe and tobacco pouch, a favorite knife or weapon, perhaps a few small dishes for use on the short journey ahead.[6]

When Beargrease died, his family buried him in Beaver Bay's Indian Cemetery, a small, inconspicuous plot atop a rise in back of the town. Several members of the Beaver Bay Anishinabe community were already buried there. A traditional cemetery lodge originally marked the location of his grave. The cemetery lodges were like little houses, formed either of lumber or of hewn logs and roofed with birchbark strips. Similar structures marked several other graves in the cemetery.[7] The little houses had small openings like windows at which visitors to the gravesite might leave a token for the dead. In keeping with the Anishinabe custom, the family would have raised a bright colored flag set on a pole above Beargrease's grave house to show the world that the man lying there was a chief, the son of chiefs.[8]

In later years, long after the grave houses had vanished and long after the local Anishinabe had vanished, the people of Beaver Bay put up white wooden crosses to mark the gravesite, but the cemetery was quickly overgrown and nearly forgotten. In 1932, the Lake County Historical Society placed a modest bronze plaque, set in concrete, to mark the site and remember those whose bones are beneath the soil. The plaque reads, "This tablet marks the location of an old Indian cemetery begun about 1865 in which are buried the following..." It then goes on to list twenty-two names, including Narcise Wishcop (John's brother-in-law), Lizzie Wishcop (John's niece), Cecelia Bluesky (John's niece), Liza Wishcop (John's neice), Antoine Beargrease (John's first son), Aikiin Beargrease (John's son Ahin), Marian Boyer (John's mother-in-law), Joe Beargrease (John's son), Nancy Beargrease (John's mother) and John Beargrease himself. Most of the names recorded are burials from after the turn of the century. The names of men and women buried in the early years of the Beaver Bay Indian community were never recorded. John's father Moquabimetem was likely buried there as well, along with the rest of the early Beaver Bay Ojibwe.

The cemetery is still there, up a little hill behind the Holiday Station in Beaver Bay. The grounds are mostly untended out of respect for Anishinabe tradition, but the cemetery draws several visitors even today. In some years, the race rules required mushers participating in the John Beargrease Sled Dog Marathon to stop in Beaver Bay and pay their respects at the cemetery by leaving a token gift of tobacco.

John's Family at Grand Marais

Shortly after his death, the Beargrease family left Beaver Bay. Except for John's younger brother Joseph, most of the remaining Beaver Bay Ojibwe community seems to have left as well. Mary sold her claim. Louise and the children, Mary and her son Clarence and even John's brother Peter and his family moved down the shore to Chippewa City in Grand Marais.

When Beargrease died, he left his eighteen-year-old son Joseph behind as the eldest son and apparent head of household, but the family suffered a second blow when seven months later Joseph died too, leaving Louise with Mabel, George and Francis. In addition to her own children, Mrs. Beargrease also took custody of her granddaughter Angeline Louise Decker, Charlotte's daughter. The 1912 Census of Chippewa Indians at Grand Portage lists Angeline as an orphan in the care of the Beargrease home, so we may assume that Herbert also had died by then. Mary and baby Clarence had moved in with Louise as well.

By relocating to Chippewa City, Louise and Mary were at least closer to Constance (Augusta) and her young family, but adding sorrow to sorrow, Constance died in the flu epidemic of 1912, leaving behind her husband John Lemier, her four-year-old son John Cyrus and her two-year-old daughter Elinor Louise.[9] Mrs. Beargrease took them in too, adding them to the growing collection of Beargrease grandchildren that filled her home.

The names of the children in Louise's Beargrease brood all appear in the Grand Portage Census records and the Grand Marais Public School records from 1912-1918. In 1915, the teen-age Mabel Louise left school to take a job. The extra income would have been a big help for the struggling clan, but it didn't last. She fell sick and died that same year.[10] In 1916, Mary had a second son by Jacob Morrison, a member of the local Anishinabe community. They named the child Constantine Francis Morrison, but he died in October of 1916.[11] Those were hard times, and funerals followed one after another.

On the Path of Souls

In 1918 the entire country was ravaged by an influenza epidemic. The Beargrease home in Grand Marais was particularly hard hit. Mrs. Beargrease "worked night and day in taking care of the other members of the household, until finally she was completely exhausted and had to give in. She was confined to her bed but a short time before death came."[12] Her own case of influenza had progressed into pneumonia. She died on December 11, 1918. Her last surviving son, seventeen-year-old George and her brother-in-law Peter were also struggling under the combined weight of the flu and pneumonia. They both died the next day. The obituary in the *Cook County Herald News* related, "All three were buried at the same time, making a very sad sight indeed. The funeral took place last Saturday and internment was made in the Catholic cemetery in Chippewa village where they were laid in the same grave. The funeral was strictly private, only a few of the nearest relatives being present at the grave."[13]

Among those present at the grave would have been the widowed Cecile (Wishcop) Beargrease, her son Peter Jr. and Louise's surviving brothers. John Lemier, Constance's widower husband was there with his two children. Of John and Louise's own children, only Mary and Nancy still survived. Nancy was thirteen years old that year. Mary was there with her son Clarence and her niece, Charlotte's daughter Angeline.

In 1919, Mary obtained land from the U.S. Government and moved to Superior, Wisconsin.[14] She died, still unmarried, in 1923 at Saint Mary's Hospital in Duluth after suffering with some form of pneumonia for two weeks. At the time, John Lemier, Constance's widower husband was also living in Superior with his two children John Cyrus and Elinor Louise. Lemier attempted to sell a parcel of his deceased wife's allotted land to help pay for transferring Mary's remains back to Grand Marais for burial with the rest of the family,[15] but Mary was interned in the Calvary Cemetery on April 14.[16]

So it is that John Beargrease's bones rest with some of the children in the Beaver Bay Indian cemetery while the bones of his beloved wife Louise lie with the other children (excepting Mary) in the Chippewa City cemetery of Grand Marais. Beargrease was ever traveling back and forth between those two villages.

Today, Beargrease descendents come through the lines of his daughter Nancy and his grandchildren Angeline Louise Decker and Elinor Louise. Of all the Beargrease children, little Nancy turned out to be the real survivor. After Mary left Grand Marais, she was the last of John's children on the North Shore. She grew up in Chippewa City, perhaps living with her aunt Cecile. According to her daughter Viola Keyport, when John Scott Mercer, the sheriff of Grand Marais grew weary of arresting the young, headstrong Indian woman for violating segregation laws, he decided to marry her. They had ten children together. She remained on the North Shore all her life. Her daughter Viola Keyport provided documents and photographs for the research of this book. Nancy lived until 1956. She was the very last of John Beargrease's children to walk the Path of Souls.

A woman once went into a trance for a day-and-a-half. When she awoke, she said that she had been to the ghost land where the northern lights are shining. She said that the dance of the northern lights is actually the ghosts rising and falling in the steps of a dance. The women there were dressed in brightly colored clothes, the men adorned as if for war.[17] Even Nanaboozhoo dwells now in that land, and so they dance in that place, where the northern lights are always shining.

That's the way it was over there, with those Anishinabe who lived at the mouth of the Little Cedar River, Eshquabe Moquabimetem and his kin. That's how it was with those folks beside the Great Lake, Kitchi Gami, while waves washed the shore and lights danced in the sky.

Epilogue

Each year, John Beargrease and his dogs run the old mail trail again in spirit. At the starting line of the annual John Beargrease Sled Dog Marathon, track officials begin the race with a ceremonial send-off for Beargrease and his team. The officials designate the first participant to leave the finish line as team number two, trailing behind the ghost of John Beargrease.

Bibliography of Material Cited

Albinson, Elmer. "Swedish Pioneer on the North Shore." *American-Swedish Institute Bulletin*. vol. 18 [17], No. 2 (Autumn, 1963).

Anderhagen, Anna. "John Beargrease, 1858-1910." vol. 1, 2003. Collection of sources and notes for MHS History players production. Minnesota Historical Society, Saint Paul, MN.

"Beargrease Cemetery." A transcription by Pat Zankman, Cook County Historical Society Administrator, originally translated from a document entitled "The Cloquet Mission, Cloquet 1905-1967." Cook County Historical Society Archives, Grand Marais, MN.

Banning, Wm. Culkins. "Beaver Bay." Minnesota Historical Society Library, Saint Paul, MN.

"Beaver Bay." Three typewritten leaves describing the founding of Beaver Bay. Minnesota Historical Society Library, Saint Paul, MN.

"The Beaver Bay Post Office" Exhibit text from Lake County Historical Society, 1950, Lake County Historical Society, Two Harbors, MN.

Bishop, Hugh E. *By Water and Rail: A History of Lake County, Minnesota.* Duluth, MN: Lake Superior Port Cities, 2000.

Cambell, Jim. "Jottings by Jim," *Two Harbors Chronicle & Times*, July 31, 1958.

Cameron, Don. *Keeper of the Town.* Superior, WI: Savage Press, 1996.

Cary, Bob and de Marcken, Gail. *Born to Pull.* Duluth, MN: Pfeifer-Hamilton Publishers, 1999.

Chester, Albert Huntington. "Explorations of the iron regions of Northern Minnesota, during the years 1875 and 1880, 1902." Minnesota Historical Society Library, Saint Paul, MN.

Christiansen, Charles P. "Snowshoes made by John Beargrease, 1977." Paper presented to Lake County Historical Society. Collected with John Beargrease File. Lake County Historical Society Archives, Two Harbors, MN.

Clark, Thomas. Diary, Thomas Clark Papers. Minnesota Historical Society Library, Saint Paul, MN.

Davis, Jessie. *Beaver Bay: Original North Shore Village.* Silver Bay, MN: Bay Area Historical Society, 2004.

Densmore, Frances. *Chippewa Customs.* Saint Paul, MN: Minnesota Historical Society Press, 1979.

Dwan, Dennis. "Growth of the Postal System on the North Shore, 1933." Minnesota Historical Society Library, Saint Paul, MN.

Eklund, Nels. "Narrative Family History of Nels Eklund, 1963." Minnesota Historical Society Library, Saint Paul, MN.

Fessler, Bert. "The North Shore in 1890, A paper read at the Annual Meeting of the Tri-County Historical Assembly, Held at Grand Portage, August 23, 1930." Minnesota Historical Society Library, Saint Paul, MN.

"Fergus Falls State Hospital Case Books, 1899-1900." Minnesota Historical Society Library, Saint Paul, MN.

Fradenburg, A. G. "Mail Saga." *Cook County News-Herald*, July 10, 1941.

Fritzen, John. *North Shore Historical Map*. Duluth, MN: Saint Louis Historical Society, 1970.

Garrison, Elizabeth. "Excerpt of Interview About Her Uncle John Slater." Collected with John Beargrease File. Lake County Historical Society Archives, Two Harbors, MN.

Gilman, Carolyn. *The Grand Portage Story*. Saint Paul, MN: Minnesota Historical Society Press, 1992.

Greve, Edward. *The Development of Lake County, MN*. Superior, WI: University of Wisconsin. 1978.

Gumtow, Vickie (Chupurdia). "Beargrease History Not Forgotten." *Lake County News-Chronicle*, January 13, 1988

"John Beargrease." Collected with John Beargrease File. Lake County Historical Society Archives, Two Harbors, MN.

"John Beargrease File—Annual dinner invitation." Collected with John Beargrease File. Lake County Historical Society Archives, Two Harbors, MN.

"John Beargrease: Out of the Past, 76 years ago [1908]." *Lake County News-Chronicle*, September 5, 1984

Kohl, Johann Georg. *Kitchi-Gami: Life Among the Lake Superior Ojibway*. Saint Paul, MN: Minnesota Historical Society Press, 1985.

Lambert, Bernard J. *Shepherd of the Wilderness: A Biography of Bishop Frederic Baraga*. L'Anse Michigan: Book Concern, 1967.

McLean, R. B. *Reminiscences of Early Days at the Head of the Lakes*. n.p. 1913.

Musicant, Ivan. "The Minnesota Seaport." Roots. No. 6, 1977.

Nute, Grace Lee. *Lake Superior*. Minneapolis, MN: University of Minnesota Press. 2000.

Peacock, Thomas D. *A Forever Story: The people and Community of the Fond du Lac Reservation*. Cloquet, MN: Fond du Lac Band of Lake Superior Chippewa, 1998.

Perich, Shawn. *The North Shore, A Four Season Guide to Minnesota's Favorite Destination*. Duluth, MN: Pfeifer-Hamilton Publishers, 1992.

Raff, Willis H. *Pioneers in the Wilderness: Minnesota's Cook County, Grand Marais and the Gunflint in the 19th Century*. Grand Marais, MN: Cook County Historical Society, 1999.

Reagan, Albert B. "A Progressive Bois Fort Indian: Ben D. Beargrease." *The Red Man*. 6, no. 6. (1914): 232-233.

Scott, William E. "Mrs. Betzler—a Beaver Bay Pioneer, 1952." Minnesota Historical Society Library, Saint Paul, MN.

Schiller, Judi and Richard. "Sled Dogs and Mushers." *Crooked Creek Observer*, February 11, 1997 [periodical on-line]; available from www.emily.net/~schiller/mushing.html ; (accessed January 26, 2006).

Sivertson, Howard, *Tales of the Old North Shore: Paintings and Companion Stories*. Duluth, MN: Lake Superior Port Cities. 1996.

Skillings, Helen Wieland. *We're Standing on Iron! The Story of the Five Wieland Brothers*. (Duluth: St. Louis County Historical Society, 1972), 33.

Tall Trees & Deep Waters: A History of East Lake County. Silver Bay, MN: Bay Area Historical Society, 1991.

Two Harbors 100 Years. Two Harbors, MN: Two Harbors Centennial Commission in coordination with the Lake County Historical Society. 1983.

Slater, Mary Louise Updegrove. "Articles about Beaver Bay, Minnesota." Minnesota Historical Society Library, Saint Paul, MN.

Tormondsen, Chris. *Tofte: A Collections of Facts and Tales of the North Shore Area of Lake Superior*. Minneapolis: Hayward Court Brief Print. 1968.

U.S. Department of the Interior, United States Land Office, Duluth, MN. Document Number 01942, "Martin Steinman vs. Mary Ann Beargrease," August, 31, 1909. Minnesota Historical Society Library, Saint Paul, MN.

Wieland, Otto E. "Some Facts and Incidents of North Shore History." (paper read at Ninth Annual Tri-County North Shore Historical Assembly meeting, Memorial Hall, Court House, Duluth, 4 September 1937). Minnesota Historical Society Library, Saint Paul, MN.

_____ "U.S. Mail on the North Shore." Minnesota Historical Society Library, Saint Paul, MN.

Wieland, Henry P. "Short History of the Wielands, 1933." North East Minnesota Historical Center Library, Duluth, MN.

Williams, Elise Sonju. "Homesteading on the North Shore, 1975." Iron Range Resource Center Library, Chisholm, MN.

Correspondence:

Beargrease Indian to Vermillion Indian Agent. 13 December 1883. Nett Lake / Bois Forte Reservation Archives, Bois Forte Heritage Center, Tower, MN.

La Pointe Indian Agent to J. T. Gregory Eag., 1886. Nett Lake / Bois Forte Reservation Archives, Bois Forte Heritage Center, Tower, MN.

Superintendent, Consolidated Chippewa Indian Agency to John Lemier. 21 May 1923. Provided to author by Sharon Johnson.

Chippewa Lake Superior Indian Agent, SN Clark, Superior, WI to Commissioner of Indian Affairs, E. S. Parker, Washington D.C., 19 December 1870, Bois Forte Heritage Center Tribal Archives, Tower, MN.

Bois Forte Historian, J. Kay Davis, to author, 17 March 2005.

Bay Area Historical Society President Ed Maki Jr., to author, 9 February 2005.

Endnotes

Chapter One

1   McLean, R. B. *Reminiscences of Early Days at the Head of the Lakes.* (n.p. 1913), 1.

2   Ibid.

3   In his *Reminiscences*, McLean has confused his late September trip to Grand Marais with a subsequent trip he made with Thomas Clark in October. McLean recalls this trip as taking place in September, but according to Clark's journal, McLean's trip with both Clark and Battise (Jean Baptiste) did not begin until October 17, two or three weeks later. In addition McLean reports encountering Godfrey at Grand Marais, but in Clark's journal, an encounter with Godfrey takes place just down the shore from Agate Bay, "one week from Grand Marais." McLean also reports exploring the Beaver River with Clark, an incident Clark recorded in his journal on October 29-30. McLean must have made an initial trip to Grand Marais in late September, and then a second trip in late October. While writing his memoirs, the two trips merged in his memory.

4   Thomas Clark, Diary 1854, Thomas Clark Papers. Minnesota Historical Society Library, Saint Paul, MN, October 22, 1854.

5   Clark's Diary, October 20, 1854, 12.

6   Ibid., October 21, 1854, 12.

7   Ibid., October 26, 1854, 17.

8   Ibid., October 27, 1854, 17.

9   Ibid., October, 28, 1854, 19.

10 McLean, 3-4.

11 Clark's Diary, October 29, 1854, 19.

12 Ibid.

13 Peet's diary is quoted in Hellen Skillings, *We're Standing on Iron! The Story of the Five Wieland Brothers* (Duluth: St. Louis County Historical Society, 1972), 10.

14 Jessie Davis, *Beaver Bay: Original North Shore Village* (Silver Bay, MN: Bay Area Historical Society, 2004) 33.

15 Helen Skillings, *We're Standing on Iron! The Story of the Five Wieland Brothers* (Duluth: St. Louis County Historical Society, 1972), 33.

16 Otto E. Wieland, "Some Facts and Incidents of North Shore History" (paper read at Ninth Annual Tri-County North Shore Historical Assembly meeting, Memorial Hall, Court House, Duluth, 4 September 1937) Articles on St. Louis County History, Minnesota Historical Society Library, Saint Paul, MN, 1937, 6.

17 Carolyn Gilman, *The Grand Portage Story,* (Saint Paul, MN: Minnesota Historical Society Press, 1992) 110.

18 Henry P. Wieland, "Short History of the Wielands." North East Minnesota Historical Center, Duluth, MN, 1933, 2.

19 Davis, 36.

20 Skillings, 36.

21 Wieland, "Short History of the Wielands," 2.

22 Otto E. Wieland, "Some Facts and Incidents of North Shore History," Articles on St. Louis County History, Minnesota Historical Society Library, Saint Paul, MN, 1937, 7.

23 Skillings, 38.

24 Ibid., 35.

25 William E. Scott, *"Mrs. Betzler—a Beaver Bay Pioneer,"* Minnesota Historical Society Library, Saint Paul, MN, 1952.

26 Wm. Culkins Banning, "Beaver Bay," Minnesota Historical Society Library, Saint Paul, MN.

27 *Duluth Minnesotian*, December 24, 1870, cited by Skillings, 39.

28 Wieland, "Short History of the Wielands," 2.

29 Davis, inside cover.

30 Wieland, "Short History of the Wielands," 2-3.

Chapter Two

1 Gilman, 1992, 110.

2 Correspondence Chippewa Lake Superior Indian Agent, SN Clark, Superior, WI to Commissioner of Indian Affairs, E. S. Parker, Washington D.C., December 19, 1870, Bois Forte Heritage Center Tribal Archives, Tower, MN.

3 Warren Upham, *Minnesota Place Names, A Geographical Encyclopedia*, [book on-line] (Saint Paul, MN: Minnesota Historical Society Press, 2001, accessed January 26, 2006); available from http://mnplaces.mnhs.org ; Internet.

4 SN Clark letter to E. S. Parker.

5 Frequently *Moquabimette*.

6 According to the Fergus Falls State Hospital record on the chief's daughter, Mrs. Bluesky, both of her parents were born in the Rainy Lake district. "Fergus Falls State Hospital Case Books, 1899-1900," Minnesota Historical Society Library, Saint Paul, MN.

7 J. Kay Davis, email correspondence with author, March 17, 2005.

8 Mahjeheshig married two wives and fathered John (who is sometimes confused with the famous mail-carrier by the same name), Ben (Tahbankenung), Kikem Joe, Mike (Baybahkahquayjew), Arthur, Alex, Julia, Theresa, Nancy, Celia and Lizzie. This large Beargrease clan eventually settled at Stony Brook, later dubbed Brookston, a small village not far from Prairie Lake where they were originally discovered. At the death of Mahjeheshig, his son Ben Beargrease became chief and was recognized as such among the Anishinabe of the Fond du Lac and Bois Forte bands. Mahjeheshig's descendents still reside in the Cloquet area under the name Beargrease. See Albert B. Reagan, "A Progressive Bois Fort Indian—Ben D. Beargrease," The Red Man. Vol. 6:6 (February, 1914): 232-233; Nels Eklund, "Narrative Family History of Nels Eklund, 1963," Minnesota Historical Society Library, Saint Paul, MN, 9.

9 The two families stayed in contact with each other. The September 19, 1908 edition of the *Lake County Advocate* reported, "Mike Beargrease, of Krogston, Minnesota, was visiting relatives at Beaver Bay this week."

10 Skillings, 34.

11 Johann Georg Kohl, *Kitchi-Gami: Life Among the Lake Superior Ojibway*. (Saint Paul, MN: Minnesota Historical Society Press, 1985) 111.

12 Skillings, 34.

13 Davis refers to her as Otoe. A Bay Area Historical Society genealogy of the Beargrease family identifies Newigagamibig as the mother of John and Bebease, but erroneously also lists her as the mother of Ben, Mike and Peter. Ben and Mike were sons of Chief Mahjeheshig and his wife Ogahbayosayquay. According to the 1875 State Census, Peter was the son of Moquabimetem and a woman named Eshegamigan. However, a Nett Lake probate record (Allotment 480) provided by Viola Keyport, a granddaughter of John, identifies Peter's mother as Ped-way-way-cum-ig-e-nung. Furthermore, Francis Beargrease, John's daughter, is listed in that record as Ped-way-way-cum-ig-e-nung's granddaughter. If accurate, this would imply that Ped-way-way-cum-ig-e-nung is the mother of both John and Peter. Ped-way-way-cum-ig-e-nung may be another name for Newigagamibig, but the probate letter lists her date of death as November 1908. John's mother died in June of 1907.

14 *Cincinnati Daily*, January 19, 1843.

15 H. P. Wieland quoted in Skillings, 37. Wieland recollects this event as happening in 1870, but this can only be an approximation. Beargrease was not yet in Beaver Bay by 1870. Carrie Hangartner was born in 1867 and recalled the incident in vivid detail, suggesting a latter date. The incident must have occurred sometime closer to 1875.

16 Born in 1867.

17 *Two Harbors, 100 Years.* (Two Harbors, MN: Two Harbors Centennial Commission in coordination with the Lake County Historical Society. 1983), 202, which relates the incident incorrectly to the son, John.

18 Skilling, 34-35.

19 Kohl, 66-67.

20 Edward Greve, *The Development of Lake County, MN* (Superior, WI: University of Wisconsin, 1978), 45-46.

21 The 1900 Federal Census lists his birth as July of 1872. The 1895 Census is in error when it lists his age as 30.

22 Information in the table is based primarily on census data, Bay Area Historical Society's genealogy, Grand Portage rolls and available death certificates.

23 Greve, 26-27.

24 Thomas D. Peacock, *A Forever Story: The People and Community of the Fond du Lac Reservation*, (Cloquet, MN: Fond du Lac Band of Lake Superior Chippewa, 1998).

25 E.g. *Two Harbors Iron Port*, December 27, 1890.

26 Anna Anderhagen, "John Beargrease, 1858-1910," A Collection of Notes and Documents on John Beargrease Compiled for the Minnesota History Players Production, Minnesota Historical Society, Saint Paul, MN.

27 Fergus Falls State Hospital Case Books, 1899-1900.

28 Davis, 91.

29 Skillings, 36.

30 Skillings, 26.

31 Charles P. Christiansen, "Snowshoes made by John Beargrease," Lake County Historical Society, 1977, Two Harbors, MN.

32 *Two Harbors Iron News*, January 31, 1908.

33 Skillings, 34.

34 Beargrease Indian to Lake Vermillion Indian agent, December 13, 1883, Bois Forte Heritage Center Tribal Archives, Tower, MN.

35 Fergus Falls State Hospital Case Books, 1899-1900 record on Peter Beargrease, Minnesota Historical Society Library, Saint Paul, MN.

Chapter Three

1 Willis H. Raff, *Pioneers in the Wilderness: Minnesota's Cook County, Grand Marais and the Gunflint in the 19th Century*, (Grand Marais, MN: Cook County Historical Society, 1999) 295.

2 *Superior Chronicle*, July 12, 1856.

3 Otto E. Wieland, "U.S. Mail on the North Shore," Articles on St. Louis County History, Minnesota Historical Society Library, Saint Paul, MN.

4 Wieland, "Some Facts and Incidents of North Shore History," 3.

5 Skillings, 31, states that the Wielands retained the star route contract for twenty-seven years after Clark relinquished it.

6 Raff points out (295) that the Lake County Board minutes from 1875 report making payments to "Mail carrier McLean" for delivering supplies at express rates.

7 Skillings, 31.

8 Wieland, "U.S. Mail on the North Shore."

9 Mary L. Emmons to Solan J. Buck, November 2, 1927 filed with "Information Relating to Alsa Alda Parker Family, 1927, 1931," Minnesota Historical Society Library, Saint Paul, MN.

10 Wieland, "Short History of the Wielands."

11 Wieland, "U.S. Mail on the North Shore."

12 Ibid.

13 Wieland, "Short History of the Wielands."

14 *Duluth Morning*, May 2, 1871.

15 Raff, 17.

16 Vickie Gumtow (Chupurdia), "Beargrease History Not Forgotten," *Lake County News Herald*, July 13, 1988. According to John's obituary, he carried the mail for eighteen years, which would suggest that he began in 1882.

17 Raff, 14, 296.

18 Ibid., 296.

19 Ibid., 296.

Chapter Four

1 *Two Harbors, 100 Years*, 202.

2 William Stein of Two Harbors, as quoted in Don Cameron's, *Keeper of the Town* (Superior, WI: Savage Press, 1996), 85.

3 The 1865 state census shows Marianne and Joseph "Wishgob" living in Beaver Bay with their son and two daughters.

4 Davis, 34.

5 Frances Densmore, *Chippewa Customs*, (Saint Paul, MN: Minnesota Historical Society

Press, 1979) 72.

6   In the 1880 Federal Census, Louise is still at home with her family as late as June.

7   Kohl, 273; Densmore, 54-57.

8   In 1883 the Wieland brothers sold their lumber company, mill and practically the entire town of Beaver Bay to the Gibbs and Mallet lumber company of Michigan. Gibbs and Mallet became the landlord of virtually everyone in town. In 1890, Ben Fesler reported finding three white families and four Indian families residing in Beaver Bay proper. He said, "No one who lives here owns the property in which he resides. It is all owned by a lumber company in Saginaw, Michigan." Bert Fessler, "The North Shore in 1890, a paper read at the Annual Meeting of the Tri-County Historical Assembly, Held at Grand Portage, August 23, 1930," Minnesota Historical Society Library, Saint Paul, MN.

9   Davis, 36.

10 Davis, 36.

11 Kohl, 6-7.

12 In obvious conflict to this record, the Lake County Historical Society records a George Beargrease born December 29, 1899, but this must be an error arising from confusion between John George Beargrease and George Beargrease who was born in 1901.

13 Kohl, 6.

14 Kohl, 276-277.

15 Davis, 67.

16 A reservation teacher to J. T. Gregory Eag, U.S. Indian Agent, Ashland, WI, January 16, 1886, Bois Forte Heritage Center Tribal Archives, Tower, MN.

17 Cameron, 85.

18 Davis, 59.

Chapter Five

1   Kohl, 39.

2   Kohl, 432-433.

3   Chris Tormondsen, *Tofte: A Collections of Facts and Tales of the North Shore Area of Lake Superior.* (Minneapolis: Hayward Court Brief Print, 1968), 25-26.

4   Dennis Dwan, "Growth of the Postal System on the North Shore," Minnesota Historical Society Library, August 21, 1933, 8-9.

5   An "Old Settler's" reminiscence in *Two Harbors Iron Port Advocate*, December 29, 1909.

6   Anna Anderhagen, "John Beargrease, 1858-1910" Vol. 1. (Saint Paul, MN: Minnesota Historical Society).

7   *Two Harbors, 100 Years*, 202.

8   Christensen, "Snowshoes made by John Beargrease."

9   Anderhagen, "John Beargrease, 1858-1910" Vol. 1. (Saint Paul, MN: Minnesota Historical Society).

10 *Cook County Herald*, April 7, 1900.

11 *Two Harbors Iron Port*, December 27, 1890.

12 Raff, 297.

13 Bob Cary and Gail de Marcken, *Born to Pull* (Duluth: Pfeifer-Hamilton, 1999), 4.

14 Carrie Brunes' memoirs, Raff, 95-96.

15 Davis, 59.

16 Ed Maki Jr., president of the Bay Area Historical Society to author, February 9, 2005.

17 Wieland, "U.S. Mail on the North Shore."

18 Bernard J. Lambert, *Shepherd of the Wilderness* (L'Anse, Michigan: Bernard J. Lambert, 1967), 174.

19 An "Old Settler's" reminiscence in *Two Harbors Iron Port Advocate*, December 29, 1909.

20 Kohl, 432-433.

21 Raff, 302, January 17, 1907 *Cook County Herald*.

22 Raff, 333.

23 "John Beargrease File—Annual Dinner Invitation," Lake County Historical Society, Two Harbors, MN.

24 A. G. Fradenburg, "Mail Saga," *Cook County News-Herald*, July 10, 1941.

25 "The Beargrease Trail—First North Shore Road," *Cook County News-Herald*, August 12, 1976.

26 Raff, 83-84.

27 Raff, 79-80.

28 *Cook County Herald*, November 11, 1893.

29 Elmer Albinson, "Swedish Pioneer on the North Shore," *American-Swedish Institute Bulletin* (Autumn, 1963), 12.

30 Raff, 83.

31 Raff, 302.

32 This story was told in the *Cook County Herald* around the turn of the century, but I have lost the reference.

33 Raff, 233.

34 *Lake County Advocate*, May 9, 1908.

Chapter Six

1 *Two Harbors Iron Port*, December 27, 1890.

2 Otto E. Wieland, "U.S. Mail on the North Shore," Articles on St. Louis County History, Minnesota Historical Society Library, Saint Paul, MN.

3 *Two Harbors, 100 Years*, 82.

4 Shawn Perich, *The North Shore, A Four Season Guide to Minnesota's Favorite Destination*, (Duluth, MN: Pfeifer-Hamilton Publishers, 1992), 37.

5 Warren Upham,. *Minnesota Place Names, A Geographical Encyclopedia*, [book on-line] (Saint Paul, MN: Minnesota Historical Society Press, 2001, accessed January 26, 2006); available from http://mnplaces.mnhs.org; Internet.

6 John Fritzen, *North Shore Historical Map*, (Duluth, MN: Saint Louis Historical Society, 1970).

7 Skillings, 37.

8 Vickie Gumtow (Chupurdia), "Beargrease History Not Forgotten," *Lake County News-Chronicle*, January 13, 1988.

9   Fritzen, *North Shore Historical Map.*

10 Lambert, 171-173.

11 Fritzen, *North Shore Historical Map.*

12 *Cook County Herald*, November 30, 1895.

13 *Cook County Herald*, December 16, 1893; March 31, 1894.

14 December 27, 1890.

15 The June 4, 1891 edition of the *Iron Port* speculated, "George Hogobone, of this place, will probably take the contract for carrying the mail between Two Harbors and Grand Portage."

16 A reprint from 1892 in the January 31, 1908 edition of the *Two Harbors Iron News* says that John was "toting the mails to and fro between Two Harbors and Beaver Bay." Perhaps he was able to subcontract that portion of the route.

Chapter Seven

1   September 10, 1891.

2   Davis, 53.

3   *Lax Lake County Advocate*, January 2, 1909.

4   Eklund, 11. The Eklund history describes Ojibwe trapping techniques as practiced by relatives of John Beargrease from the Cloquet, MN area.

5   *Two Harbors, 100 Years*, 202.

6   Davis, 76-77.

7   Minnesota Legislature. Special Laws of Minnesota for 1866, Chapter 98.

8   Fergus Falls State Hospital Case Books, 1899-1901 record on Peter Beargrease, Minnesota Historical Society Library, Saint Paul, MN.

9   *Two Harbors, 100 Years*, 202.

10 *Lake County Advocate*, February 1, 1908.

11 Raff (p. 232) notes the first bounties paid in Cook County were set at $7.50 per wolf.

12 Elise Sonju Williams, *"Homesteading on the North Shore."* (Chisholm, MN: Iron Range Resource Center Library, 1975), 2.

13 Judi and Richard Schiller, "Sled Dogs and Mushers," *Crooked Creek Observer*, February 11, 1997 [periodical on-line]; available from www.emily.net/~schiller/mushing.html (accessed January 26, 2006). Schiller quotes a fragment from the journal of a man named Harold Strang, a great-uncle of a neighbor of Judi Schiller. Mrs. Schiller, the author of the article, borrowed the journal one night and copied the passage down, assuming it was about John Beargrease of Beaver Bay. Unfortunately, since the passage is removed from its original context and the owner of the complete diary is no longer to be found, it is impossible to be certain. It seems more probable that the John Beargrease character in the Strang journal is not John Beargrease of Beaver Bay, but John Beargrease [son of Mahjeheshig] the sibling of Mike and Ben Beargrease from the Cloquet/Fond du Lac area, close relatives of the Beaver Bay Beargrease Indians. According to Nels Eklund's reminiscence (p. 10), the Cloquet area John Beargrease "was a very tall, strong, good looking Indian. He was the one who brought in venison for us in the early years."

14 Williams, 2.

15 Raff, 80.

16 Albinson.

17 Ivan Musicant, "The Minnesota Seaport," Roots 6, 1977.

18 *By Water and Rail*, 69.

19 Gilman, 95.

20 Kohl, 453-454.

21 Bert Fesler, "The North Shore in 1890, A paper read at the Annual Meeting of the Tri-County Historical Assembly, Held at Grand Portage, August 23, 1930," Minnesota Historical Society Library, Saint Paul, MN.

22 In Fesler's list, John's name appears after the Good Harbor Bay names like Mathias Johnson and C. Hanson. Based on Fesler's linear method of recording names down the shore, this might lead one to conclude that Beargrease was fishing out of Hovland. But as Raff points out (p. 70), Johnson and Hanson moved into cabins in Grand Marais every summer, returning to their homes at Good Harbor only after the fishing season was over. Fesler probably encountered them along with Beargrease in Grand Marais and recorded them all as Grand Marais fishermen.

23 Fesler Diary, August 7, 1890, "The North Shore in 1890."

24 Fesler, "The North Shore in 1890."

25 Hugh E. Bishop, *By Water and Rail: A History of Lake County, Minnesota* (Duluth, MN: Lake Superior Port Cities, 2000), 69.

26 Bishop, 77.

27 *Two Harbors Iron News*, May 23, 1899.

28 *Two Harbors Iron Port*, October 31, 1891.

29 *Cook County Herald*, November 1894, cited by Raff, 300.

30 September 22, 1894.

Chapter Eight

1   Tormondsen, 25.

2   *Cook County Herald*, January 13, 1894.

3   For example, in November of 1897, John brought him to Two Harbors in the mail boat, but he returned on the *Dixon* (*Iron Trade Journal*, November 18, 1897).

4   *Cook County Herald*, December 12, 1896.

5   *Cook County Herald*, February 6; April 16, 23, 1897.

6   "John Beargrease's north shore mail contract expires May 15th when the Dixon will carry it." (*Two Harbors Iron News*, April 30, 1897).

7   *Cook County Herald*, December 11, 1897.

8   *Cook County Herald*, September 25, 1897.

9   *Two Harbors Iron Trade Journal*, November 4, 1897.

10 *Cook County Herald*, August 7, 1897.

11 *Two Harbors Iron Trade Journal*, January 12, 1898.

12 *Two Harbors Iron News*, November 26, 1897.

13 *Two Harbors Iron Trade Journal*, December 16, 1897.

14 *Cook County Herald*, January 8, 1898. Raff, 110-111.

15 January 21, 1898.

16   *Two Harbors Iron Trade Journal* quoted in *Cook County Herald*, January 22, 1898.

17   Raff, 303.

18   Howard Sivertson, *Tales of the Old North Shore: Paintings and Companion Stories.* (Duluth, MN: Lake Superior Port Cities, 1996).

19   "The Beaver Bay Post Office," Exhibit text from Lake County Historical Society, 1950, Lake County Historical Society, Two Harbors, MN.

20   "John Beargrease File—Annual dinner invitation," Lake County Historical Society, Two Harbors, MN.

21   Raff, 329.

22   *Two Harbors Chronicle & Times*, July 31, 1958.

23   Raff, 329.

24   *Cook County Herald*, March 1898, reprinted in the *Two Harbors Iron Trade Journal*, March 31, 1898.

25   *Two Harbors Iron News* July 22, 1898.

26   *Two Harbors Iron Trade Journal*, November 25, 1898.

27   *Cook County Herald*, December 10, 1898.

28   Catherine Kirby Jones Diary, January 5, 1899, as quoted by Raff, 303.

29   *Cook County Herald*, January 14, 1899.

30   "Hovland Locals," *Cook County Herald*, January 14, 1899.

31   Catherine Kirby Jones Diary, January 14, 1899, as quoted by Raff, 303.

32   *Cook County Herald*, February 4, 1899.

33   *Cook County Herald*, February 3, 1899.

34   *Cook County Herald*, February 18, 1899.

35   *Cook County Herald*, February 18, 1899.

36   *Cook County Herald*, March 4, 1899.

37   *Cook County Herald*, March 11, 1899.

38   March 25, 1899.

39   Greeve, 26-27.

40   *Cook County Herald*, April 1, 1899.

41   *Cook County Herald*, April 1, 1899, quoting a Two Harbors Newspaper.

42   *Cook County Herald*, April 8, 1899.

43   Catherine Kirby Jones Diary, April 12, 1899, as quoted by Raff, 303; and in an online article, "Turn of the Century Visitors to Chippewa City," www.boreal.org/compage/history/chipcity.html; (accessed February 17, 2006).

44   *Two Harbors Iron News*, December 1, 15, 1899; Cook County Herald, December 23, 1899.

45   *Two Harbors Iron News*, October 6, 1899.

Chapter Nine

1   Lake County Warranty Timber Deed, October 11, 1899, on display at Bay Area Historical Society. John's land is described as "the fractional west half of the northwest quarter and the fractional north half of the southwest quarter of section nineteen in Township 56 north of range seven, West of the Fourth Principal Meridian, containing

one hundred and sixty and acres, more or less, according to the Government survey thereof."

2   *Two Harbors Iron News*, November 24, 1899.

3   Fergus Falls State Hospital Case Books, 1899-1900 record on Mrs. Bluesky, Minnesota Historical Society Library, Saint Paul, MN.

4   Fergus Falls State Hospital Case Books, 1899-1900 record on Peter Beargrease, Minnesota Historical Society Library, Saint Paul, MN.

5   Davis, 31.

6   Tormondsen, 25-26.

7   Elise Sonju Williams, *"Homesteading on the North Shore"* (Chisholm, MN: Iron Range Resource Center Library, 1975), 2.

8   Davis, 51.

9   Christiansen, "Snowshoes made by John Beargrease."

10 Elise Sonju Williams, *"Homesteading on the North Shore"* (Chisholm, MN: Iron Range Resource Center Library, 1975), 2.

11 U.S. Department of the Interior, United States Land Office, Duluth, MN. Document Number 01942, "Martin Steinman vs. Mary Ann Beargrease," August, 31, 1909. (Saint Paul, MN: Minnesota Historical Society Library). Also, *Lake County News-Chronicle*, January 13, 1988.

12 U.S. Department of the Interior, United States Land Office, Duluth, MN. Document Number 01942, "Martin Steinman vs. Mary Ann Beargrease," August, 31, 1909. (Saint Paul, MN: Minnesota Historical Society Library).

13 *Tall Trees & Deep Waters: A History of East Lake County* (Silver Bay, MN: Bay Area Historical Society, 1991), 12.

14 Ibid.

15 *Lake County Advocate*, May 4, 1907.

16 In 1909 the paper merged with A. Delacy Wood's *Two Harbors Iron Port*.

17 *Lake County Advocate*, April 13, 1907.

18 U.S. Department of the Interior, United States Land Office, Duluth, MN. Document Number 01942, "Martin Steinman vs. Mary Ann Beargrease," August, 31, 1909 (Saint Paul, MN: Minnesota Historical Society Library).

19 *Cook County Herald*, May 4, 1907.

20 *Lake County Advocate*, May 11, 1907.

21 *Lake County Advocate*, June 1, 1907.

22 They lived in the rooms in the Bramer building on Monroe Street. *Cook County Herald*, June 22, 1907.

23 *Lake County Advocate*, June 15, 1907.

24 *Lake County Advocate*, June 15, 1907.

25 *Lake County Advocate*, June 8, 1907.

26 *Lake County Advocate*, June 15, 1907.

27 Mrs. Slater, her son and a Miss Bixbee. *Lake County Advocate*, August 3, 1907.

28 *Lake County Advocate*, August 10, 1907.

29 *Lake County Advocate*, August 17, 1907.

30 *Lake County Advocate*, August 17, 1907.

31 *Lake County Advocate*, September 7, 1907.

32 In addition, Peter, Cecile and their son Peter Jr. were living under the same roof.

33 *Duluth News Tribune* article reprinted in *Two Harbors Iron News*, January 24, 1908.

34 "Record of Certificates of Conviction in Justices of the Peace Courts, Lake County, 1903-1913." (Saint Paul, MN: Minnesota Historical Society Library), 6.

35 *Duluth News Tribune* article reprinted in *Two Harbors Iron News,* January 24, 1908.

36 *Lake County Advocate*, February 15, 1908.

37 *Lake County Advocate*, April 4, 1908.

38 *Two Harbors Iron News*, December 25, 1908.

39 "Out of the Past, 76 years ago, 1908," *Lake County News-Chronicle*, September 5, 1984.

40 Probably the Elizabeth Slater family. See photo caption in Davis, *Beaver Bay, Original North Shore Village*, which pictures Mary Beargrease and Elizabeth Slater and her daughter, stating that Mary often worked for Mrs. Slater.

41 *Lake County Advocate*, October 24, 1908.

42 Bishop, 16. Nevertheless, Carrie Hangartner, her oldest daughter, recalled how the family took in Chief Beargrease after his scuffle with the bear. He stayed in their home several days while they nursed him back to health.

43 Mary Louise Updegrove Slater, "Articles about Beaver Bay, Minnesota, The Hangartner Family, [undated]," Minnesota Historical Society Library, Saint Paul, MN, 4.

44 *Lake County Advocate*, November 28, 1908.

45 *Lake County Advocate*, 1909.

46 Gumtow (Chupurdia), "Beargrease History Not Forgotten" *Lake County News-Chronicle,* January 13, 1988.

47 Slater, 4.

48 Williams, 3.

49 Williams, 3.

Chapter Ten

1 Densmore, 99.

2 February 6, 1909.

3 The apocryphal version can be traced back to Greve who must have misunderstood the LaPlante letter.

4 Edward LaPlante to the Lake County Historical Society, excerpt in notes of "Descendents of John Beargrease," a Lake County Historical Society document in the Anderhagen collection.

5 *Two Harbors Iron Port Advocate*, July 6, 1910.

6 Densmore, 73-74.

7 Davis, 101.

8 Kohl, 373.

9 "Beargrease Cemetery," a transcription by Pat Zankman, Cook County Historical Society Administrator, originally translated from a document entitled "The Cloquet Mission, Cloquet 1905-1967." (Grand Marais, MN: Cook County Historical Society Archives).

10 "Grand Portage, MN Superintendency Annual School Census Report, 1916" (Ander-hagen Collection, Saint Paul, MN: Minnesota Historical Society).

11 "Beargrease Cemetery" (Grand Marais, MN: Cook County Historical Society Archives).

12 *Cook County News Herald*, December 11, 1918.

13 *Cook County News Herald*, December 18, 1918.

14 Gumtow (Chupurdia), "Beargrease History Not Forgotten," *Lake County News Herald*, July 13, 1988.

15 Superintendent, Consolidated Chippewa Indian Agency to John Lemiere. 21 May, 1923. Provided to author by Sharon Johnson.

16 Mary Beargrease Death Certificate, Saint Louis County. (Saint Paul, MN: Minnesota Historical Society Library). Mary's son Clarence William Hangartner died on March 10, 1940 in Saint Louis County. According to Minnesota birth and death records, he married a Rose Neumainville and had at least one surviving son by the name of William Elmer Hangartner, who, in turn, lived until 1977 and may have living descendents today.

17 Densmore, 74.

ABOUT THE AUTHOR

Daniel Lancaster studied literature and creative writing at Southwest State University in Marshall, Minn. and completed a BA in literature at Metropolitan State University in St. Paul, Minn. He has been a contributor to various publications and periodicals in the fields of religious studies, early Christianity and Judaism. He has lived in St. Paul with his wife, Maria, and their four children since 1992.

CPSIA information can be obtained
at www.ICGtesting.com
Printed in the USA
FFHW020817140119
50116492-54996FF